DAMASCUS STEEL
Theory and Practice

Gunther Löbach

4880 Lower Valley Road • Atglen, PA 19310

Other Schiffer Books on Related Subjects:

Forging Damascus Steel Knives for Beginners, 978-0-7643-4012-3, $24.99

Copyright © 2013 by Schiffer Publishing, Ltd.

Originally published as *Damaszenerstahl Theorie und Praxis* by Wieland Verlag GmbH. Translated from the German by Ingrid Elser with Dr. John Guess, editorial advisor, and technical guidance by Gunther Löbach.

Cover Design by RoS
Photos by Gunther Löbach (unless attributed otherwise)

Library of Congress Control Number: 2012955711

All rights reserved. No part of this work may be reproduced or used in any form or by any means—graphic, electronic, or mechanical, including photocopying or information storage and retrieval systems—without written permission from the publisher.
The scanning, uploading and distribution of this book or any part thereof via the Internet or via any other means without the permission of the publisher is illegal and punishable by law. Please purchase only authorized editions and do not participate in or encourage the electronic piracy of copyrighted materials.
"Schiffer," "Schiffer Publishing, Ltd. & Design," and the "Design of pen and inkwell" are registered trademarks of Schiffer Publishing, Ltd.

Type set in Zurich BT

ISBN: 978-0-7643-4294-3
Printed in China

Published by Schiffer Publishing, Ltd.
4880 Lower Valley Road
Atglen, PA 19310
Phone: (610) 593-1777; Fax: (610) 593-2002
E-mail: Info@schifferbooks.com

For our complete selection of fine books on this and related subjects, please visit our website at www.schifferbooks.com. You may also write for a free catalog.

This book may be purchased from the publisher. Please try your bookstore first.

We are always looking for people to write books on new and related subjects. If you have an idea for a book, please contact us at proposals@schifferbooks.com.

Schiffer Publishing's titles are available at special discounts for bulk purchases for sales promotions or premiums. Special editions, including personalized covers, corporate imprints, and excerpts can be created in large quantities for special needs. For more information, contact the publisher.

In Europe, Schiffer books are distributed by
Bushwood Books
6 Marksbury Ave.
Kew Gardens
Surrey TW9 4JF England
Phone: 44 (0) 20 8392 8585; Fax: 44 (0) 20 8392 9876
E-mail: info@bushwoodbooks.co.uk
Website: www.bushwoodbooks.co.uk

For my parents
Otty and Bernd

Contents

Preface		8
Introduction: The Myth of Damascus Steel		10

Part I: Theory — 14

1	**Types of Damascus**	**16**
1.1	Welded Damascus	16
1.2	Powder Metallurgy Formed Damascus	16
1.3	Crucible Damascus (Wootz)	19
1.4	Similar Materials and Techniques	21
1.4.1	Refined Steel	21
1.4.2	False Damascus	21
1.4.3	Damascening	23
1.4.4	*Mokume Gane*	23
1.4.5	Timascus	24
1.4.6	Dambrascus	25
1.4.7	Superconductive Wiring	25
2	**Origin and History**	**27**
2.1	Ancient Times (800 B.C. to 600 A.D.)	27
2.2	Middle Ages (600 to 1500 A.D.)	29
2.3	Modern Times (1500 to 1800 A.D.)	30
2.4	The Nineteenth Century	31
2.5	The Twentieth Century	33
2.6	The Twenty-first Century	33
3	**Aesthetic Appearance**	**36**
3.1	Fundamental Parallels	36
3.1.1	Stone	36
3.1.2	Wood	36
3.1.3	Metal	39
3.1.4	Glass	39
3.1.5	Animal Materials	39
3.1.6	Food	39
3.2	Visual Parallels / Associations	40
3.3	Design Possibilities	41
3.3.1	Color and Contrast	41
3.3.2	Texture	42
3.3.3	Shape and Pattern	42
3.3.4	Combinations with other Materials and Techniques	43
4	**Patterns in Damascus Steel**	**44**
4.1	Laminate	46
4.2	Mosaics	47

Contents

4.2.1	Bitmap Mosaic	47
4.2.2	Spirograph Mosaic	48
4.2.3	Matrix Mosaic	49
4.2.4	Jigsaw Mosaic	50
4.2.5	Mosaic from Finished Parts	51
4.3	Orientation	52
4.4	Multiplication	53
4.5	Twisting	55
4.5.1	Combining Several Twisted Bars	56
4.5.2	Phases of Grinding	56
4.6	Surface Manipulation	58
4.6.1	Embossing Technique	58
4.6.2	Notching Technique	58
4.7	Deformation	60
4.8	Unfolding	61
4.9	Cover Layer / Multiple Bars	63
4.9.1	Composite Blades	64
4.9.2	"Wyrmfāh" Damascus	66
4.10	Inlays	67
4.11	Gallery of Damascus Steel Art	68

	Part II: Practice	**74**
5	**Damascus in Practice**	**76**
5.1	Many Ways to the Destination	76
5.2	Safety at Work	78
5.2.1	Forge Welding	78
5.2.2	Grinding / Polishing	78
5.2.3	Working with Acids	79
6	**Materials**	**80**
6.1	Carbon Content	80
6.1.1	Welding Qualities	80
6.1.2	Carbon Diffusion	81
6.1.3	Colors / Shading	81
6.2	Other Alloying Elements	81
6.2.1	Manganese	81
6.2.2	Nickel	81
6.2.3	Chromium	82
6.3	Commonly Used Materials	82
6.3.1	Tool Steel O2	82

Contents

6.3.2	1070 and 1095	82
6.3.3	File Steel W2	82
6.3.4	Ball Bearing Steel 52100	82
6.3.5	Spring Steel AISI 9255	82
6.3.6	Mild Steel	82
6.3.7	15N20	83
6.3.8	L6	83
6.3.9	Pure Nickel	83
7	**Heat Sources**	**84**
7.1	Coal Forge	84
7.2	Gas Forge	86
7.3	Electric Oven	88
8	**Power Sources**	**90**
8.1	Handheld Hammer	90
8.2	Power Hammer	90
8.3	Hydraulic Press	91
8.4	Other Possibilities	92
9	**Auxiliary Materials**	**93**
9.1	Flux	93
9.1.1	Glass Sand (Silicon Dioxide SiO_2)	93
9.1.2	Borax (Disodium Tetraborate $Na_2[B_4O_5(OH)_4]$)	93
9.1.3	Mixtures and Additives	94
9.2	Etching Substances	94
9.2.1	Ferric Chloride ($FeCl_3$)	94
9.2.2	Sulfuric Acid (H_2SO_4)	94
9.2.3	Citric Acid ($C_6H_8O_7$)	95
10	**Preparing the Billet**	**96**
10.1	Dimensions of the Billet	96
10.2	Number of Layers and Their Arrangement	98
10.3	Preparing the Surfaces	99
10.4	Fixing & Adding a Handle	102
11	**Forge Welding**	**106**
11.1	Pre-Heating the Billet	106
11.2	Applying the Flux	107
11.3	"Packing"	108
11.4	Heating to Welding Temperature	110
11.5	Welding	112
11.6	Checking the Weld	114
11.7	Welding Flaws	115
11.7.1	Prevention of Flaws	115
11.7.2	Correcting Flaws	116

Contents

12	**Mosaics**	118
12.1	Bitmap Mosaic	118
12.2	Spirograph Mosaic	120
12.3	Matrix Mosaic	122
12.4	Jigsaw Mosaic	124
12.5	Mosaics from Finished Parts	125
12.5.1	Cable Damascus	125
12.5.2	Machine Chain Mosaic	127
13	**Multiplication**	129
13.1	Planning	132
13.2	Drawing Out	133
13.3	Next Steps	133
14	**Twisting**	134
14.1	Preparation	134
14.2	Twisting the Bar	136
14.3	Next Steps	138
15	**Surface Manipulation**	140
15.1	Embossing Techniques	140
15.2	Notching Techniques	144
16	**Deformation**	148
16.1	Explosion Pattern Damascus	148

17	**Unfolding**	154
18	**Pattern Combinations**	156
18.1	Cover Layer Technique	156
18.2	Multiple Bar Technique	156
18.3	Inlay Technique	157
19	**Working with Damascus**	159
19.1	Forging	159
19.1	Cutting	160
19.3	Soft Annealing	161
19.4	Machining	163
19.5	Grinding	164
19.6	Hardening & Annealing	166
19.7	Etching	167
19.8	Care & Maintenance	169

Epilogue	170

Appendix 171

Materials and Heat Treatment	171
Bibliography	172
Index	172

Preface

I clearly remember the hot summer day that a couple of fellow students from HAWK University of Applied Science and Arts (Hochschule für Angewandte Wissenschaft und Kunst, Hildesheim, Germany) and I made our first attempts with Damascus steel under the guidance of Hartwig Gerbracht, head of the workshop. Billets of mild steel and O2 burnt up because we only had a rudimentary understanding of creating and maintaining correct temperatures. We made errors while welding, welds came loose, and we burned holes in our clothes. But all this was forgotten when we etched the first successfully welded billet and the fine pattern we had hoped for became visible.

Starting with this first, small success, I developed a fascination for this material, which remains unbroken and has continued to grow. To understand it, create it, and shape it according to my own ideas became a real obsession.

In the beginning, I hardly knew about the wide variety of possibilities and the many branches of science hidden behind Damascus. In time I discovered more and more new aspects through related literature and conversations with experienced Damascus smiths. I found many fascinating aspects and traits that make this material so versatile and interesting: history, material quality, types of steel, the ability to create patterns, heat treatment, surface treatment, etching techniques, and last but not least, the possibilities with respect to design. As described in the following, the great number of influential factors leads to almost immeasurable variations; on the one hand, this offers a lot of possibilities, but on the other, makes it almost impossible to grasp a complete understanding of this material.

Thus it is the goal of this book to provide a broad base of knowledge about Damascus steel in a clear, organized way. It ought to be the foundation on which knowledge in various areas can be deepened through further research and experimentation.

In the first part of the book, I look at Damascus steel from a theoretical level and address history, classification of types, and various common patterns. In the second part of the book, I build on the theory behind Damascus steel to offer a practical manual for working with this fascinating material. Here I introduce production, creation of patterns, and various treatments of welded Damascus.

Preface

The practice of creating and working on crucible Damascus (wootz) is not part of this book, as this area has very different requirements with respect to equipment, knowledge, and patience, and is not recommended for beginners.

My special thanks go to Achim Wirtz, who enabled the publication of this book through a multitude of tips, facts, and images. I also want to thank the following people, who all helped in one way or another to create this book: Aliki Apoussidou, Per Bilgren, Prof. Werner Bünck, Joel Davis, Christian Deminie, Richard van Dijk, Hartwig Gerbracht, Ulrich Gerfin, Dr. Barbara Grotkamp-Schepers, Manfred Heiser, Lutz Hoffmeister, Robert Kaufmann, Mick Maxen, Chad Nichols, Gene Osborn, Martin Steinhorst, Peter J. Stienen, Jean-José Tritz, and Dr. Hartwin Weber.

Gunther Löbach

The author can be reached via his homepage www.ScorpioDesign.de.

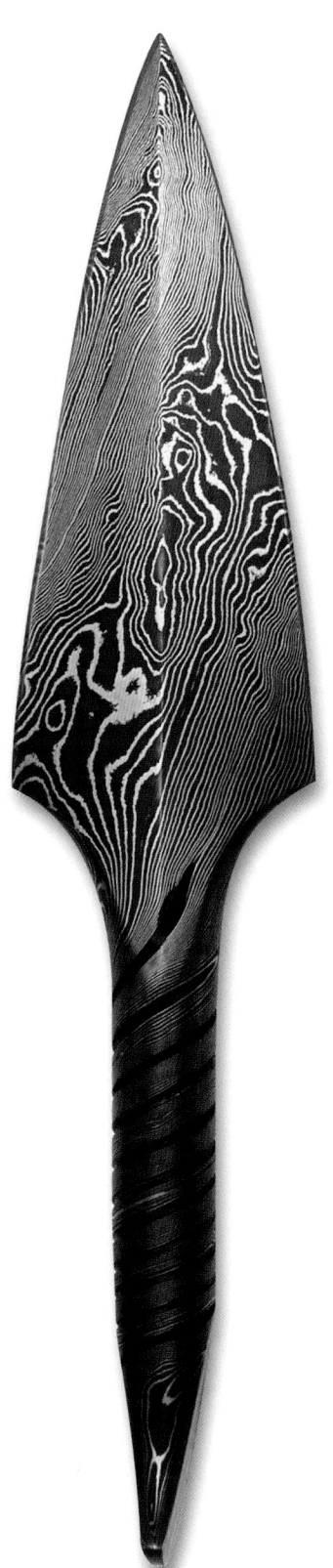

Introduction: The Myth of Damascus Steel

The Myth of Damascus Steel

A multitude of myths and half-truths is spun around Damascus steel and its characteristic appearance. The reason for this is partially due to the diversity and complexity of the topic and various obscure sources, but it is also the result of a series of pseudo-scientific television documentaries. The big secretive fuss surrounding Damascus steel also has economic reasons: Naturally, the people who know most about this material are the ones who produce and market it themselves. But these people rarely have an interest in taking the magic away from the myth (which goes a long way to promoting successful sales).

In the following, a few of the most commonly spread legends and obscurities are mentioned briefly and, where necessary, corrected. Where more detailed information is available about a specific topic later in this book, I offer chapter references.

What Exactly is Damascus Steel?

Damascus steel is inhomogeneous steel. This means there is an unequal distribution of the contained alloying elements (e.g., carbon, manganese, nickel). This state can be achieved in two different ways: either pieces of two or more steels of different grades are combined to form one block (see "1.1 Welded Damascus," or "1.2 Powder Metallurgy Formed Damascus") or, under certain circumstances, a segregation takes place inside a piece of melted steel (see "1.3 Crucible Damascus").

The zones of different composition also differ with respect to corrosion, depending on the alloying elements. The areas which are not high-alloyed are attacked more strongly. When treating the polished Damascus steel with acid, characteristic patterns show up due to this effect, and a relief structure can be created.

The various kinds of Damascus steel are described in chapter 1.

Was Damascus Steel Invented in Damascus?

No. Neither welded Damascus nor crucible Damascus was invented in the Syrian metropolis. But for many centuries, Damascus was an important trading center for all kinds of goods. Historians assume that the expression "Damascus steel" became established because weapons made from this material were traded here in large numbers, and thus were associated with the city by people in many places. In chapter 2 I show the historical development of Damascus steel. The abbreviated form "Damascus" nowadays is used more often, and both expressions are used in this book with identical meaning.

How Much "Magic" Is Used in the Production of Damascus?

None. In earlier times, the smiths and their working techniques might have been surrounded by secrets because their knowledge and know-how, with respect to producing and treating the steel, seemed like pure magic to their contemporaries. The darkened workshop (for better visibility of the heat colors) and the murmuring of verses (to measure the duration of single work steps) surely added to this.

In our times, few people believe in magic, and so there are different reasons why there is myth surrounding the production of Damascus. Most people believe—rightly so—that the incomprehensible production process can be

Introduction: The Myth of Damascus Steel

explained by science and thus works without any magic. But because we are aware of the enormous achievements of modern industrial production, therein lies fascination with the possibility to create, using nothing more than fire and hammer—archaic and anachronistic methods—a material which in most cases possesses outstanding quality and an unusual aesthetic appearance.

Are Damascus Blades in General "Better" than Those Made from Other Steel?

No. First of all, the quality of a blade, apart from the material it is made from, is also dependent on geometry and heat treatment. But also, when looking at material quality (achievable sharpness, edge retention, flexibility), it's the properties of the raw materials being used that establish the fundamental characteristics.

Nowadays, a multitude of outstanding, standardized steels is available to the bladesmith. Many of these can be combined to create Damascus steel. Through the interaction between different materials (e. g., the movement of some alloying components), new material properties are created. In order for these properties to be as good, or even better than those of the basic materials, a skillful and knowledgeable smith must combine these materials in a sensible way. Depending on these factors, good and bad examples exist for Damascus blades and monosteels alike.

In our times, Damascus steel earns its reputation, especially for its unusual aesthetic appearance, its function as an element of design (see more about this in chapter 3.3), and the myth connected with this material.

Created with techniques closely-related to Damascus steel, so-called sandwich blades can be made to have a macroscopic compound structure, i.e., three-layer blades with a "hard," central cutting layer and outer layers of "soft"

Introduction: The Myth of Damascus Steel

material. These constructions, in general, are superior to monosteel with respect to their flexibility. Such combination techniques are often used by the same smiths who also create Damascus steel. Of course, Damascus steel can also be combined in this way.

Why Are Blades from Damascus Steel Famous for Their Quality?

They were technically superior in former times. Up to the time of industrialization, the production of high-quality steel with consistent properties was very complicated and labor-intensive. Thus the weapons of ordinary soldiers were produced from average or even inferior materials. Weapons made from Damascus steel, on the contrary, were in most cases costly and unique pieces for the aristocracy and usually were produced by very good smiths. These smiths had complete control over all aspects important to the quality of a blade: choice of material, geometry, macroscopic compound structure, and heat treatment. Besides that, only the best available steels were used for such extravagant blades. Due to these circumstances, weapons made from Damascus steel were far superior to those "mass produced" and thus highly valued, or feared, accordingly.

Introduction: The Myth of Damascus Steel

Nowadays, this advantage has vanished due to advancements in smelting techniques and the great number of standardized steel grades. With monosteels as well as Damascus, the knowledge and skill of the smith are decisive for the final quality of a blade.

What Constitutes the Myth of Damascus Nowadays?

Its exotic nature. Damascus steel, in many cases, is associated with scimitar-wielding Saracens, ancient Damascus, the *Arabian Nights*, and an oriental atmosphere in general. These common clichés are supported and visualized by movies and TV, an exotic background which really doesn't have a factual grasp on the actual historical development and geographical distribution of the material. Apart from this, the steel alone, with its distinguished pattern, also has the appeal of the unusual and the obscure.

Its diversity. Whoever delves a bit into the various kinds and patterns of Damascus steel will quickly realize that there are almost unlimited possibilities for creating this material. The great number of influential variables that contribute to the appearance of this material (see chapters 3.3 and 4) results in an enormous amount of variation, which always leaves space for discovering, testing, and experiencing new things.

Its uniqueness. Handmade Damascus steel is a "living" material because every piece looks different. The workmanship shows up like handwriting in the structure and thus in the pattern. Irregularities enhance the organic patterns and give them their unmistakable character. As there are no two pieces of wood with absolutely identical grains, each piece of this material is unique as well.

Its value. In general, Damascus steel is seen as a high quality material that should have a high price. The immense cost and effort in production, and especially the high portion of manual work in this process, results in correspondingly high selling prices.

Is Industrially Produced Damascus "Real" Damascus?

This depends on your point of view. Ever since it was possible to create Damascus steel according to industrial standards (see 1.1 and 1.2), there has been a controversial discussion about whether this type of Damascus is "real" Damascus or not. From a technical point of view, this question can easily be answered, "yes," but the industrial variety does lack some of the aforementioned aspects.

It has uniform patterns due to the standardized production process with machines, but in this way the unique character is lost. The choice of available patterns is also rather narrow, because it is uneconomical to run a large number of different production and processing methods at once.

Since the mythical aspects of Damascus steel are very important for most buyers, in the discussion about "real" or "not genuine," arguments are used like "the steel has to be heated in the fire." In my opinion, this is not aiming at the goal because here again there are many nuances—does a gas forge count as fire, or only a coal forge? Is hand-forged Damascus "not genuine" because it was heated in an electric furnace?

As you can see, a sharp, technical differentiation is hardly possible, so that in the end only the buyer and user themselves can decide on what is "real" Damascus. The buyer should make up his/her mind about which aspects are important: is the individuality of the hand-forged Damascus steel valued, or is the pattern itself of merit, regardless of the production method? This depends on one's knowledge about the specific types and their differences, but is also a matter of personal taste.

Photo: German Blade Museum, Lutz Hoffmeister

Part I: Theory
Chapter 1: Types of Damascus

Types of Damascus

There are several types of Damascus steel that all use similar materials and techniques, which can also be easily combined. Here are the different variations, imitations, and parallels.

1.1 Welded Damascus

Welded Damascus consists of pieces of two or more different grades of iron/steel. In the simplest case, these are pieces of sheet metal from two raw materials with different alloying composition which are stacked alternately, then are welded together in the forging fire. For this, they are heated up to temperatures around 2,015–2,190°F (1,100–1,200°C) and then fused by mechanical pressure (forging).

By etching the piece, the structure of the material is finally visible. The contrast in the pattern therefore is dependent on the alloying elements of the steels and their relative position in the electrochemical series. For example, nickel (bright) and manganese (dark) are two alloying components which aid forge welding and in combination produce a pronounced contrast.

Stainless steels containing chromium can't be welded using the classic method. The chromium oxide, which is created on the surface of the metals when heated, prevents the materials from fusing. These materials can only be welded with considerable technical effort to keep away oxygen (i.e., welding in an inert gas atmosphere or vacuum). There are various types of industrially manufactured, stainless and welded Damascus. Usually these are created by rolling sheet metal that has been preheated to welding temperature while the entire rolling train is housed in an inert gas atmosphere or vacuum.

The patterns created in welded Damascus can be influenced in a variety of ways, for example, by the shape of the basic materials used and by using different methods of forging. The possibilities for variations are described in detail in chapter 4.

1.2 Powder Metallurgy Formed Damascus

The powder metallurgy (PM) process follows the same principle used for welded Damascus: "pieces" of steel and alloying components are fused into one piece. The differences are the size of the metal pieces used for the process and the fact that they are fused together thermally.

In the PM process, as the name already implies, very small particles (grain sizes about 0.1 mm) are used, which are created by pulverizing liquid metal in an inert gas atmosphere. This steel powder is mixed in accordance with the desired alloy components, then fused into a block by sintering under high pressures and temperatures; this is called hot isostatic pressing (HIP).

Powder metallurgy products are distinguished by a very even and fine-grained distribution of steel components (carbides, etc.). The advantages resulting from this are that the material is extremely tough, with a significantly high breaking strength. Besides that, powder metallurgy allows for the production of parts with complex geometry, and the inherent refinement keeps finishing processes to a minimum. Another advantage is that stainless steels (containing chromium) created by using inert gas or vacuum can be welded.

Chapter 1: Types of Damascus

Types of Damascus Steel and Similar Materials

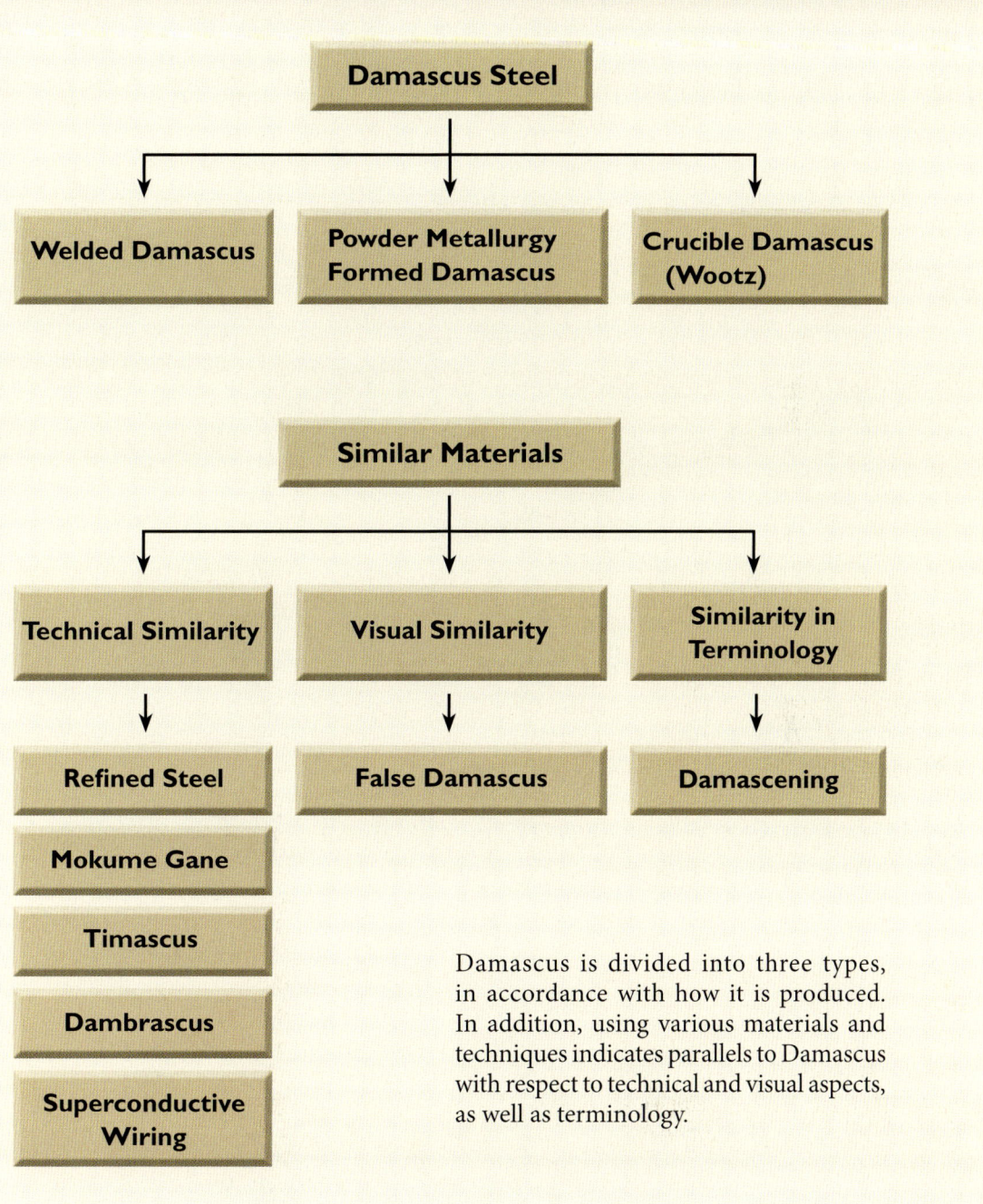

Damascus is divided into three types, in accordance with how it is produced. In addition, using various materials and techniques indicates parallels to Damascus with respect to technical and visual aspects, as well as terminology.

Chapter 1: Types of Damascus

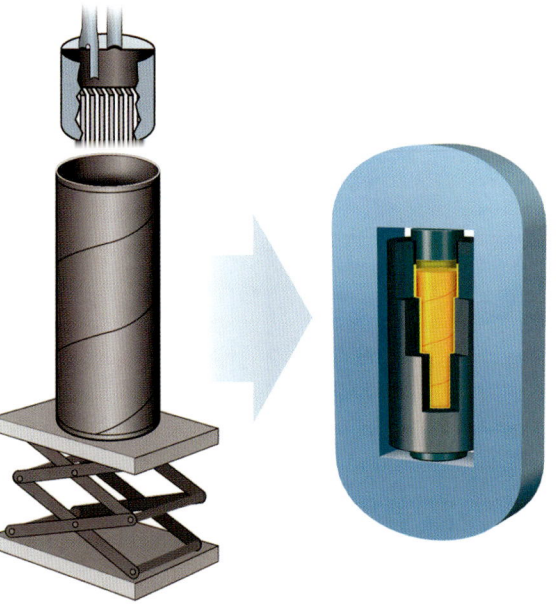

Filling in metal powder   Hot isostatic pressing (HIP)

Forge-welded Damascus is put together from individual pieces of different steel types.

PM-Damascus is produced by sintering powder of different steel types. *Images: Damasteel AB*

Chapter 1: Types of Damascus

The Swedish company Damasteel AB takes advantage of this method and arranges powder from two different grades of steel in certain patterns to create a kind of welded Damascus. They refine the blocks they produce in a conventional way by forging and rolling. Creating the patterns is handled with the same techniques as conventionally welded Damascus (see chapter 4), but on an industrial scale.

Damasteel's materials are available as semi-finished products (rods with a round or rectangular cross-section) in various patterns. The retail prices depend on the pattern and the cross-section but on average (as of May 2009) are between 400 and 600 euros per kilogram ($500–750 per 2.2 lbs).

Damasteel Damascus was developed from 1993 to 1994 and has been industrially produced since 1995. Because of its qualities (corrosion resistance and good steel quality for most applications) it is very popular in industry as well as arts and crafts. Its main use is for knife blades.

1.3 Crucible Damascus (Wootz)

This type of Damascus is mentioned as the "real" Damascus steel in many sources. Probably because this was the material bought and sold in Damascus, which was decisive in naming it. Crucible Damascus was developed much later than welded Damascus (see chapter 2).

The word *wootz* may stem from the languages of the Indian subcontinent and South Asia. According to a study by University of Halle Indologist Jürgen Hanneder, it is derived from the Sanskrit word *Vuds*, which means "high-quality iron" or "steel."

In contrast to welded Damascus, this material is not merged together from pieces of various steels but is smelted like conventional steel (thus the expression "crucible steel"). The product of this process, an ingot of characteristic shape, is called "wootz king" or "wootz cake."

Wootz has multiple special qualities, including a high carbon content (about 1.5 percent). Basically, it is a special alloy, previously only found in a certain area of India as an ore containing various alloying elements. On its surface, wootz cake displays what is called a "primary pattern." There are various reasons why this pattern is created: first, wootz steel contains very small amounts (0.003–0.02%) of molybdenum and vanadium; second, wootz has well-defined temperatures (holding and cooling times); third, the appearance of these alloys and the defined temperatures create large inhomogeneities (dendrites) that show up during slow solidification of the molten mass. This creates an unequal distribution of primary carbides, which can achieve sizes within the range of millimeters, and thus the "primary pattern."

If the material is then "kneaded" thoroughly by repeated forging, these areas (dendrites and the area in between, which solidifies last of all) are increased in length by reshaping, and the carbides are broken up. By means of long, cyclical intermediate annealing within a certain temperature range, the carbides are additionally rearranged without disturbing the macroscopic inhomogeneity. This rearrangement is enhanced by adding molybdenum and vanadium, so areas with almost homogeneously distributed carbides appear next to areas mostly free of carbides. The structure now visible on the surface is called "secondary pattern." Since the carbides that were created with much effort dissolve again at high temperatures, such a kind of annealing would destroy the Damascus pattern completely.

So, in principle, wootz is a monosteel with inhomogeneous distribution of carbides. While welded Damascus features areas with different carbon content arranged in layers, the carbon content in crucible steel interpenetrates like felt. In other words, you can imagine the carbide-rich sections as a three-dimensional web running through the steel.

Chapter 1: Types of Damascus

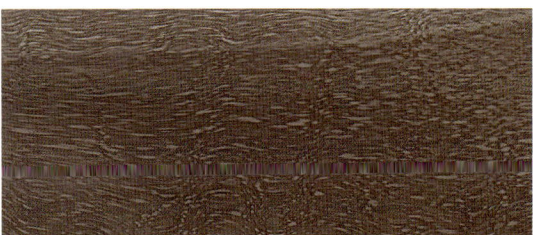

Wootz is created by melting a steel type with specific composition and a laborious forging process.
Photos: German Blade Museum, Lutz Hoffmeister (above), Achim Wirtz (right)

In this armature of refined steel, the structure (direction of "fibers") of the material is easy to recognize because of its corrosion. *From the Far North Regional Museum exhibit, New Zealand*

Refined steel is produced by multiple forge welding and drawing out the raw steel. This method ensures that the carbon content is mostly homogenized.
Photo: The Deutsches Museum, Munich

Chapter 1: Types of Damascus

The patterns of crucible Damascus are very characteristic and can hardly be copied with welded Damascus. Depending on the manufacturing process and the steel composition, coarse or fine patterns are created. These can be further changed by techniques used to manipulate the surface (see chapter 4.6), but the results are usually less distinct than with welded Damascus, because the basic material in crucible steel is more irregular. These kinds of wootz patterns created later through further manipulation are called "tertiary patterns."

1.4 Similar Materials and Techniques

In the following section I introduce more materials which have certain parallels to Damascus steel, and sometimes are mistaken for it. Some are only similar in name or have similar aesthetic looks, while others are created in a similar way and differ with respect to the materials used.

1.4.1 Refined Steel

For this kind of steel, pieces of different quality and composition are used as basic materials. But the reason for this procedure is exactly the opposite: by folding and welding many times, the steel should be homogenized in such a way that it has a consistent quality. The layers created by welding many times are so fine that they are almost invisible to the naked eye. By diffusing the carbon between the single layers, the carbon content of the material is homogenized. The specific technical and aesthetic qualities of welded Damascus are lost in this process.

This procedure was used until smelting techniques developed to the point where steel of consistent quality could be fabricated. Many times, two different qualities of refined steel were used as basic materials for welded Damascus.

Japanese swordsmiths perfected their skills in this area in such a way that it was possible for them to predict the final composition of the traditionally used sword steel (*tamahagane* or "jewel steel") by the choice and mixture of the raw building blocks. By looking at color, weight, and the appearance of fracture, they could deduce the quality and carbon content in pieces of the melted bloom (*kera*). Further information on this topic can be found in the book *The Craft of the Japanese Sword*.

1.4.2 False Damascus

Towards the end of the nineteenth century, Damascus steel was an enormously popular

A dagger with a false Damascus pattern. The border of the lithographic template is visible.
Photo: Peter J. Stienen

Chapter 1: Types of Damascus

Chapter 1: Types of Damascus

material for making knives and fire arms. As the world industrialized methods for creating this material, metal workers began to investigate how to produce good imitations on a larger scale. The solution that stuck was to make decorative etchings on the surface of monosteel that imitated the various Damascus patterns.

To create this effect, a lithographic procedure was used, whereby a masking lacquer was transferred to the metal surface. Either real Damascus patterns or patterns copied by drawing them manually were used as templates for decoration.

In this process, the material is etched in an acid bath where only the uncovered portions are corroded, revealing the pattern like a relief. To enhance the contrast, various burnishing techniques are often applied. The pattern of this false Damascus, of course, is only on the surface and doesn't have any relation to the inner structure and makeup of the steel. It can thus be removed by grinding. How "realistic" such an etched decoration appears to be depends greatly on the templates used and the burnishing techniques. Obviously there are good and bad examples of this technique.

1.4.3 Damascening

This method of decoration, which was perfected in Solingen, Germany, contains a repertoire of different etching, burnishing, and gilding techniques. It was frequently used for decorating blades, but technically has no similarity to Damascus steel.

1.4.4 *Mokume Gane*

This method of combining various non-ferrous and precious metals (copper, silver, and gold among others) as well as their alloys was developed by Denbei Shoami in Japan around 1700 A.D. In general, the structure is similar to that of welded Damascus, however, instead of steel, the aforementioned materials are used as raw materials. Three methods for fusing exist:

Pattern book with various damascening patterns.
Photo: German Blade Museum, Lutz Hoffmeister

Chapter 1: Types of Damascus

Soldering: This method leads to problems in many cases with respect to further manipulation of the material. The expansion coefficients of solder and basic materials usually differ quite drastically, which may cause the delamination of layers and the creation of cracks.

Diffusion welding with liquid phase: With this procedure the basic materials are cautiously heated until a new alloy is created in the area of contact, which is liquid due to its low melting point. It provides a unification of the metals after cooling down.

Solid-state diffusion welding: Contrary to the above technique, the materials are only heated to temperatures which are well beneath the melting points of the used metals and their common alloys. During the long heating period (eight to twelve hours) in an inert gas atmosphere, atoms of the basic metals diffuse along the boundaries into the other materials and new mixed crystals are created.

The creation of patterns for *mokume gane* is done by means of the same techniques as for welded Damascus (see chapter 4). Because of its relatively soft materials, *mokume gane* is especially suited for jewelry and the work of silversmiths. This product can't be used for tools, especially cutting tools. But in comparison with monochrome Damascus steel, it brings the aspect of color into play. In Japan, a multitude of unusual alloys are used that, by nature, or with the aid of various surface treatments, cover a broad range of hues. These offer plenty of additional possibilities to the designer.

Further information can be found in the book *Mokume Gane*.

1.4.5 Timascus

This material was developed by the Americans Chuck Bybee, Bill Cottrell, and Tom Ferry

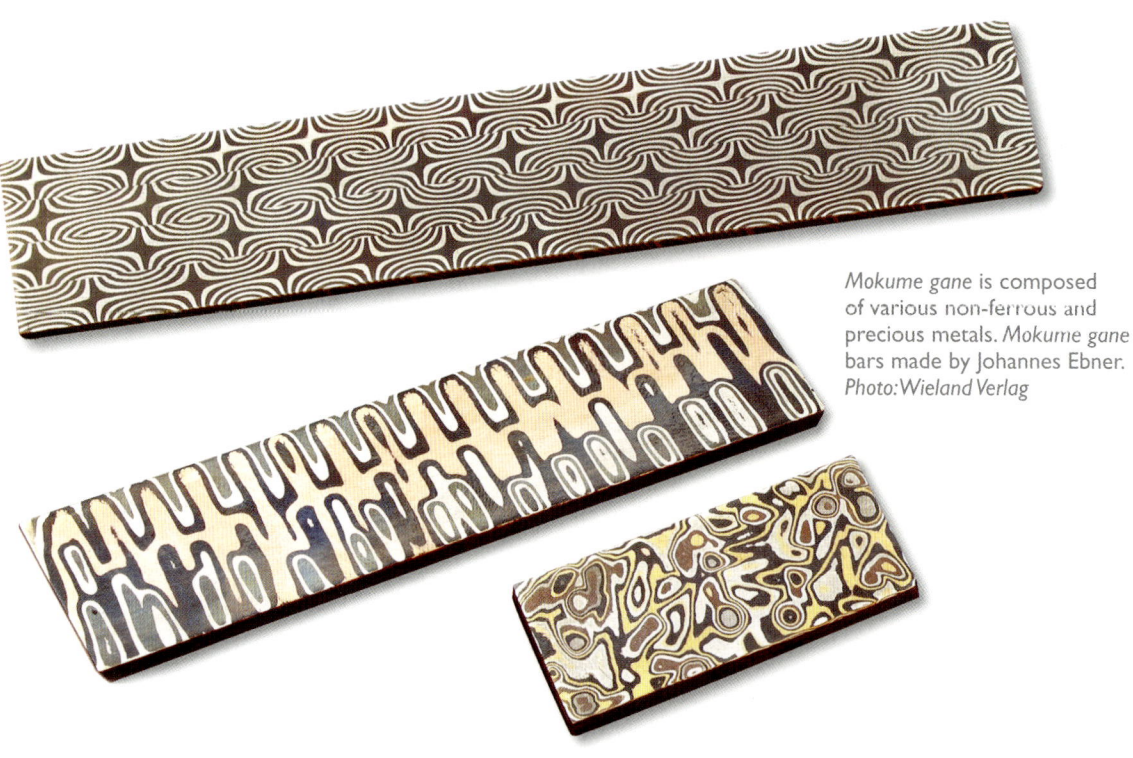

Mokume gane is composed of various non-ferrous and precious metals. *Mokume gane* bars made by Johannes Ebner. Photo: Wieland Verlag

in 2002. For the first time, they succeeded in fusing layers of different titanium alloys by forge welding. The exact procedure is their well-kept secret, but there are enough objects made from timascus to indicate that the process is easily duplicated.

The appeal of this titanium-titanium-compound lies in the fact that the individual alloys react in different ways during thermal coloring or anodizing, and thus a palette of intense colors can be achieved. Moreover, timascus of course has the advantages of ordinary titanium: it is relatively lightweight and extremely resistant to corrosion. The calculated retail price lies between $1,200 and $2,000 per kilogram (as of November 2008).

1.4.6 Dambrascus

The name of this material is derived from brass. It is a composite of steel and brass, which is produced in an unusual way: part of a steel cable is heated to a yellow color and then submerged in a crucible with molten brass. The liquid metal enters through the pores of the steel cable and bonds with it. Afterwards, you can continue to work on the piece as you would normally.

Based on a traditional technique in which holes in coarse Damascus were filled with molten non-ferreous metals, the American Gene Osborne developed this method in 1994. It represents a combination of Damascus steel and *mokume gane* techniques.

1.4.7 Superconductive Wiring

The methods for producing superconductive wires for use in high-energy electromagnets have certain parallels to the creation of welded Damascus. These wires are used, for example, in magnetic resonance tomographs, particle accelerators (colliders), and (perhaps in the future) fusion reactors. With these materials, however, it's not the mechanical properties, but the electrical qualities that determine the production of the composite. The wires consist of several leads of a niobium alloy, the actual superconductor. These are embedded in a surrounding matrix of copper, with the purpose of abducting the electrical current after the breakdown of superconductivity (after reaching the critical temperature) without destroying the coil. In some cases an additional shielding layer is necessary between superconductor and matrix to reduce eddy currents inside the matrix. For this, mostly copper-nickel alloys are used. First, the wires are welded as a billet (bolt) by means of extrusion, then drawn out to a length of several kilometers with diameters in the range of millimeters. At that stage the thickness of the veins is in the range of micrometers.

Timascus is a compound of different titanium alloys that achieve marked color contrasts by anodizing or thermal coloring. Folding knives by Hans Weinmüller. *Photo: Wieland Verlag*

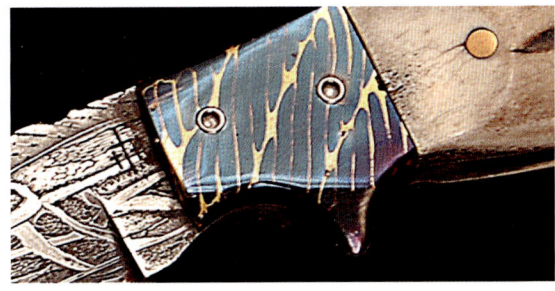

Dambrascus is made from a steel cable whose pores are filled with molten brass. Knife bolsters of blued dambrascus by Gene Osborn. *Photo: Gene Osborn*

Chapter 1: Types of Damascus

Superconductive wiring is made from a compound of niobium and copper. It is shown here at different stages of production. The diameters (clockwise from top left) are: 220 mm, 50 mm, 5 mm, and 0.1 mm. *Photo: Dr. Hartwin Weber*

Chapter 2: Origin and History

Origin and History

As with so many inventions throughout mankind's history, the driving force behind Damascus steel was the development of military technology—the search for weapons superior to those of the enemy. In the case of Damascus steel, where and when this technique was first used can't be determined definitely. Like iron processing in general, it seems that welded Damascus was developed in several places simultaneously. The oldest finds of welded Damascus date back to about 300–400 B.C. (La Tène period).

Through far-reaching trade and various mass migrations, the genesis of this material is blurred even further. Besides that, sources are diffuse or even contradictory. Nevertheless, I will try to point out the most important milestones, in chronological order.

2.1 Ancient Times (800 B.C. to 600 A.D.)

In the beginnings of iron processing, only the bloomery furnace was known as a means for extraction—a brick lined furnace, charged with charcoal, inside which iron ore was melted. The products of this process differed greatly with respect to the carbon content and the purity of the iron.

In addition, only small pieces of the resulting bloom could be used, which limited the size of the finished products. Only the invention of forge welding made it possible for the smiths to combine several of these pieces to create larger objects.

During the next phase smiths realized that, especially for blades, a laminate of "soft" and

Because of corrosion, the Damascus pattern of this ancient sword blade is visible. *Photo: German Blade Museum, Solingen, Lutz Hoffmeister*

Chapter 2: Origin and History

About 350 B.C. Europe
The oldest forge-welded Damascus finds are from the La Tène period. The technique spread over wide areas of Europe, especially during Roman times.

200–1000 A.D. Northern Europe
Forge-welded Damascus was produced by Merovingians, Carolingians, and Vikings. Some of the blades already have very complex structures.

1750–1900 A.D. Solingen / Liège
Large amounts of forge-welded Damascus were produced in factories. Solingen mainly produced edged weapons, and Liège established itself as a center for pistol and rifle barrels.

About 100 B.C. Middle East
The production of crucible Damascus (wootz) was discovered in Persia. In the nineteenth century, certain ore deposits in India were exhausted and the technique was gradually forgotten.

About 1250 A.D. Indonesia
On Java, the fine art of forging Damascus developed. The main area of application was the traditional Indonesian dagger, the kris.

Chapter 2: Origin and History

"hard" steel created specific advantages—toughness and edge retention. Thus the first weapons of welded Damascus were created: composite blades, mostly made with a cover layer technique. Discoveries from the La Tène period (about 400–300 B.C.) began to show very complex structures.

Towards the end of the La Tène period and during the beginning of the Roman Empire, the method was further refined and a composite of different steels was used for decorating especially splendid weapons. The first blades were produced using finely layered and partially twisted welded Damascus. A definite determination of age, unfortunately, is not possible. It is assumed that the method was developed in several places (India, Persia, Middle East, Northern Europe) at the same time. This technique became known and distributed throughout the Roman Empire via smiths of tribes or nations supporting the Romans.

Remarkable in this context are the finds of Illerup Ådal in present-day Denmark. Among sacrificial offerings from the second century A.D., there are a multitude of swords with highly complex Damascus patterns containing many mosaic and inlay patterns (see chapters 4.2 and 4.10).

To produce flexible blades that were resistant to wear, in many cases a core of soft iron was used which was then coated with cover layers and cutting layers out of decorative welded Damascus. A certain structure was quite common and was produced in a similar way over many centuries: the so-called *wyrmfāh* blades were made from two or more twisted bars in the center of the blade, with cutting layers of layered Damascus (see chapter 4.9.2).

In the classic period, the production of crucible Damascus (wootz) from Indian ore spread throughout Persia. The exact date of the discovery of this process cannot be reconstructed; the oldest archaeological findings of wootz blades (Taxila, Pakistan) were dated to the first century A.D. The unique process of creating wootz mostly stayed within the circle of Arab and Persian cultures during its entire history, while Damascus welding was used by many different peoples.

2.2 Middle Ages (600 to 1500 A.D.)

In Europe, welded Damascus (usually of *wyrmfāh* composition) was used over many centuries (without many changes) by Merovingians, Carolingians, and Vikings. By the end of the twelfth century a slow decline of the production

Reconstruction of a bloomery furnace: after burning is completed, the furnace is opened and the sponge-like loop is removed.
Photo: Achim Wirtz

Chapter 2: Origin and History

An Indonesian kris with a pronounced pattern.
Photo: German Blade Museum, Solingen, Lutz Hoffmeister

started—progress in smelting steel was somewhat responsible for this. Since the quality of the melted product continually improved and in particular became more homogeneous, the technological advantage of welded Damascus vanished at the cost of its more involved production methods. Starting at the end of the thirteenth century, few blades were still made from welded Damascus.

The method of producing refined steel, long known in Europe, was discovered in Japan around the seventh century A.D. During the following centuries, the bladesmiths there achieved great expertise with respect to homogenizing the melted material and controlling its carbon content. Also in Japan, the blades received additional toughness by a macroscopic compound structure (i. e., by means of a core from soft iron).

Independent of Europe, in Japan, the Middle East, and present-day Indonesia (especially on Java), the art of producing welded Damascus was perfected. The *kris* (daggers, often with variegated flame or snake like blades), produced there since the thirteenth century, sometimes show a very fine structure of layers and high contrasts, the latter often caused by the use of meteoric iron containing nickel.

2.3 Modern Times (1500 to 1800 A.D.)

During the fourteenth and fifteenth centuries very few blades were made from welded Damascus in Europe. But from about 1550 onward, this technique experienced a renaissance. About this time more and more edged weapons were made from Damascus steel. At the beginning (during the sixteenth century) the mechanical properties of composite steels probably stood in the foreground; despite all the improvements, they were still superior to the properties of smelted steel and thus were used, especially for high-quality weapons of the aristocracy. Many edged weapons of this time were made from

Chapter 2: Origin and History

composite steels but were polished completely, and thus the pattern remained invisible.

But it didn't take long until the characteristic patterns became desirable again and they increasingly were made visible on the objects. A real fashion arose, in the course of which large numbers of splendid weapons were produced from welded Damascus. During the eighteenth century, the barrels of fire arms began to be produced with this material.

During this time, various centers for producing Damascus were established in Europe. In Solingen, mainly edged weapons were produced, and the city of Liège, Belgium, became famous for its excellent pistol and rifle barrels. Many objects of Damascus steel were also created during this time in the British city of Birmingham, and in the area of present-day Turkey.

After first replicating the classic patterns, new paths were increasingly followed and companies started to outdo each other by means with flamboyant structures. The techniques of surface manipulation (see 4.6) were perfected during this era.

2.4 The Nineteenth Century

In many places the creation of Damascus steel was done in factories, which increasingly achieved the character of industrial production. Structured rolls were used more and more to produce steel as well as the various patterns with consistent quality. Catalogs have survived from the second half of the nineteenth century from which customers could order edged weapons and fire arms, with a wide choice of standardized patterns.

As industrialization expanded, manufacturers searched for new, economical methods for fabricating Damascus, and products made from it, with machines. But it turned out that the skills and instincts of a smith could not be replaced by

A historic pattern catalog from the Carl Eickhorn company, Solingen, around 1900.
Photo: German Blade Museum, Solingen, Lutz Hoffmeister

Various edged weapons made of Damascus steel, around 1900.
Photo: German Blade Museum, Solingen, Lutz Hoffmeister

Chapter 2: Origin and History

a machine. Eventually, however, people switched over to using machines to manufacture classic Damascus steel products (edged weapons and firearms) from monosteel, because the quality and economics of monosteel had improved significantly with new smelting techniques (1885 Bessemer converter, 1864 Siemens-Martin process).

At first people could not do without the aesthetic appearance of Damascus patterns, so they imitated the material by etching decorations on monosteel products, which became very popular (see 1.4.2). This added to the threat on the already declining existence of Damascus factories and led to a larger conflict between them and the "counterfeiters." The conflict only came to an end in 1898, after a law prohibited the manufacturers and vendors from naming their decorated products "Damascus" or "Damascus steel" in any way. Nevertheless, the demand for and the number of authentic Damascus pieces produced declined more and more, and only a few years later most Damascus manufactories stopped their production.

At this time the production of crucible Damascus was also reduced in the Middle East—probably because certain deposits of iron ore in India (which contained important alloying elements, see 1.3) were depleted. At about the same time, experiments were conducted in Russia to determine the composition of wootz steel. The metallurgist P. Anossov, together with a couple of smiths, managed to create a similar material which he called "Bulat." But he wasn't able to explain why these materials possessed their characteristic qualities.

2.5 The Twentieth Century

During the first half of the twentieth century, especially in Solingen, a lot of edged weapons were produced from Damascus steel for military dignitaries and politicians. After overcoming the painful consequences of World War II, a couple of smiths started to revive this technique in the late 1960s and early 1970s.

In the United States, Daryl Meier and Bill Moran are recognized as the pioneers of modern Damascus forging: in Germany, it was Manfred Sachse and Heinz Denig. Damascus smiths were soon supported by the development of a custom knife market in the United States, which encouraged collectors and created an outlet for artisans.

This trend continues today and seems to be expanding in popularity. In fact, a significant amount of the Damascus steel produced today is processed into knife blades. While some artisans still use Damascus for jewelry and other objects, their market volume is comparatively small.

New inspiration was brought by a procedure developed in Germany in 1983 by Friedrich Schneider and Richard Hehn, which, for the first time, allowed stainless steel—steel containing chromium—to be welded in the forging fire. In 1993, the powder metallurgy method for producing welded Damascus was developed, which again created a new variation of this composite material (see 1.2).

At the same time, scientists tried to uncover the secrets of wootz steel. The Russian researchers V.P. Borsunov and V.A. Tscherbakov published a survey in 1993 with very precise analyses of historical wootz products, though no decisive discoveries were made.

2.6 The Twenty-first century

The popularity of Damascus steel endures, especially in the area of custom knives, and the number of smiths is constantly growing. What was an almost forgotten art about 50 years ago nowadays is more popular than ever before—perhaps because it is different from current mass production. From the collector's point of view, the aesthetics and the myth

Chapter 2: Origin and History

Letter openers of the early twentieth century, made by P. Müller, and others.
Photo: German Blade Museum, Solingen, Lutz Hoffmeister

connected to Damascus are enticing. The technological superiority which formerly led to its development, however, vanished with the efficiency of modern monosteels.

Spurred by historical models and the contemporary products of competitors, knifemakers are constantly exploring new patterns and material combinations. A multitude of standardized steel grades offers present-day Damascus smiths more high-quality raw material than their historical colleagues could have dreamed of. Modern tools and equipment like power hammers and gas and electric forges make the hammermen and other assistants superfluous, allowing professional smiths and hobbyists to pursue this craft on their own.

In the area of wootz research, there have recently been decisive breakthroughs. In particular, the American metallurgist J. D. Verhoeven, in cooperation with the smith A. H. Pendray, managed to create wootz and also draw conclusions on the creation of its special structure (see 1.3).

Various semi-finished Damasteel products.
Photo: Damasteel AB

Damascus-forging has become increasingly popular over the last few decades.

Dagger made of stainless Damascus by Friedrich Schneider.
Photo: Wieland Verlag

Chapter 3: Aesthetic Appearance

Aesthetic Appearance

The "mixture" of various steels per se does not cause any change in aesthetic appearance. The differences in the structure only become apparent with corrosion. This can be seen with buried objects, in that sword blades often look like real "skeletons." One kind of steel is corroded deeply and eaten away while the other is far less corroded; this creates a kind of relief like rib structure. This effect, having evolved over centuries, can be created within a short amount of time by submerging the object into an acidic bath in which one of the steels is corroded more quickly than the other.

You can speculate about the historical importance of the aesthetic appearance, but the unmistakable patterns fascinated people back then as they do today—this is documented by numerous sagas and legends. And as ever more complicated patterns were integrated into the objects, the aesthetic appearance become established as an important component. This peaked in the eighteenth and nineteenth centuries, when the characteristic material structure, with its technical advantages, was abandoned altogether for economic reasons, and the look of the Damascus pattern was imitated by etching decorations onto a monosteel (see 1.4.2).

Today, the aesthetic appearance of the material is still the main attraction. Even though there are many monosteels available to make knives that perform just as well as Damascus steel, the highest demand and price tags are placed on knives made from Damascus because of their unique aesthetics.

Below I will present some parallels to Damascus that introduce ways of thinking about and approaching pattern formation, as well as the various features and capabilities of different materials.

3.1 Fundamental Parallels

The fundamental principle of any Damascus pattern is to make the inhomogeneous structure of the material visible. The following examples are based on this principle. Some inhomogeneous structures occur in nature, others are produced by humans.

3.1.1 Stone

Various types of stone have veins running through them or contain layers of different colors or composition. A piece cut randomly from such a stone shows a pattern on its surface similar to that of Damascus steel. As its various components (soft and hard layers) eroded, the structure—which can be recognized by its color—can contain a three-dimensional relief.

Since ancient times, certain stones have been valued because of their characteristic, natural texture. Into this category fall agate, marble, malachite as well as specific kinds of jade. Layered stones with pronounced color contrast (e.g., agate, Arabian onyx, Carnelian onyx, etc.) were worked into gems about 3,000 years ago by cutting pieces with layers parallel to the visible surface. The engraving was done in such a way that the background was made from one layer (usually a darker one), with the motif standing out in color. The contrast between the layers enhanced a certain motif (or pattern)—here we can see parallels to the techniques of surface manipulation in Damascus steel (see 4.6).

3.1.2 Wood

The unique, organic texture of wood has been valued by humans since ancient times, and used for decorative purposes. Worldwide about

25,000 to 30,000 types of wood exist, of which about 3,000 to 5,000 can in theory be used on a commercial basis, with about 200 to 250 available on the market. The variety of colors, grain, and technical qualities is almost without limit.

A large number of woods are distinguished by how pronounced their grain structure is. During the yearly cycle of growth, the tree creates early wood (spring wood) and late wood (summer wood) alternately. The cells of the summer wood have smaller volumes and thicker walls, which means that their rings are usually smaller and denser than those of spring wood. For most kinds of wood, areas of late wood are darker in color. The annual rings are each made up from one section of early wood and one of late wood. These are arranged concentrically inside the tree trunk.

There are various ways to cut through wood (radially, tangentially, or perpendicular to the grain) to reveal its different structures and thus display an array of patterns. With wood you can see that there is a clear relationship between the orientation of a structure and the visible surface. Damascus steel is quite different from wood, however; as long as the welds are flawless, the mechanical stability is pretty consistent. With wood, however, the direction of the grain affects mechanical stability under load and when the material shrinks.

While the growth of the annual rings for wood is comparable to the technique for creating patterns (see chapter 4), growth defects of the wood can be compared to techniques influencing the pattern. Various influences (e. g., injuries, obstacles, environmental factors) cause interruptions or deformities in the structure, which in turn lead to interesting patterns on the surface.

The aesthetic parallels between wood and steel led to the creation of *mokume gane* (see 1.4.4), Japanese for "wood-grained metal."

Many gemstones are valued because of their patterns. Left: colored agates, right: malachite.

The pronounced layer structure of agate.

This striped jasper has layers of distinct colors.

An example of the different hardnesses in individual rock layers: one type was eroded. *Punakaiki* ("Pancake Rocks"), New Zealand

Chapter 3: Aesthetic Appearance

Different types of cuts: Radial cut...

Tangential cut...

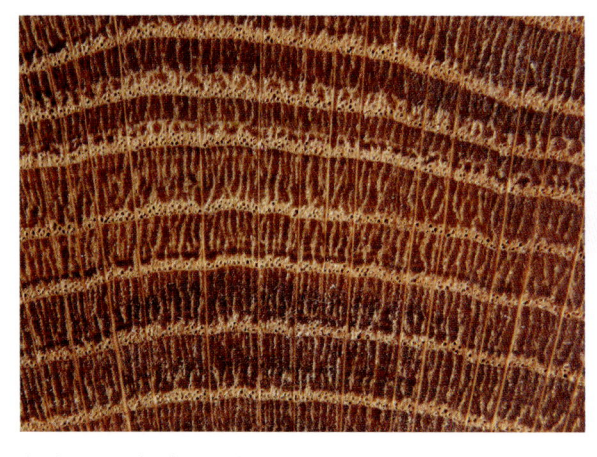

And perpendicular to the grain.

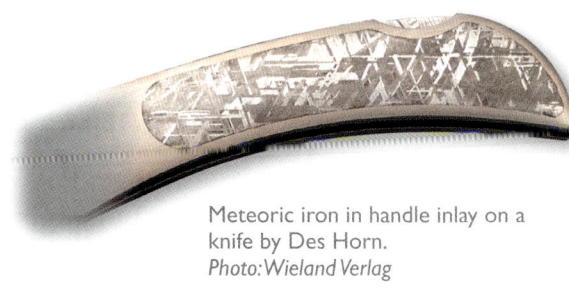

Meteoric iron in handle inlay on a knife by Des Horn.
Photo: Wieland Verlag

Millefiori beads are parts of a mosaic rod assembled from different colored glasses.

The layered structure of a shell is especially visible in cut pieces.

Chapter 3: Aesthetic Appearance

3.1.3 Metal

In metals, coarse, inhomogeneous structures form in a natural way only under specific circumstances. An example of this is the so-called Widmannstätten pattern (named after the Austrian chemist Alois von Beckh-Widmannstätten), found in certain types of meteoric iron. The special structure of coarse lamellas with different nickel content is formed when the material cools very slowly in outer space.

3.1.4 Glass

Because of its transparency, or translucency, it is possible to see the internal structure and the surface appearance of this amorphous material. By fusing glass of different colors and/or transparency, a structure is created which can afterwards be influenced by shaping. Some fields of glass art make use of this principle. Among them is the Millefiori technique, where parts of mosaic rods from colored glass are made into beads or fused to transparent glass to create flat structures. Filigree glass and reticello glass, for which colored glass threads are fused to colorless glass in certain patterns and then distorted by shaping, show parallels to Damascus steel, in this case to the matrix mosaic (see 4.2.3).

3.1.5 Animal Materials

Some natural materials from the animal kingdom have a structure similar to that of Damascus. For example, the layered structure of shells and some kinds of horns and antlers follow the same principle. Differences in color and texture in the various areas can create a wide variety of patterns, depending on how the material is cut.

3.1.6 Food

A conspicuously large variety of food receives a specific aesthetic featuring a visible inner structure. Some of these structures are created by nature (e.g., kiwifruit, marbled meat, etc.), others are created by humans (e.g., layered cake, sushi, etc.). Since almost all kinds of food are cut into pieces prior to eating, the structure along the cut surfaces can be seen and is often emphasized for aesthetic reasons. Besides differences with respect to texture, the colors of the individual components are also an important element.

Since a detailed description of the broad culinary spectrum would exceed this limited section, here is a list with a easily visualized examples:

- banana
- melon
- leek
- marble cake
- sugar cane
- crêpes
- pie
- layered cocktails
- Swiss cheese
- citrus fruit
- pomegranate
- Neapolitan ice cream
- liquorice candy
- chocolate confections
- marbled beef
- café au lait
- boiled egg

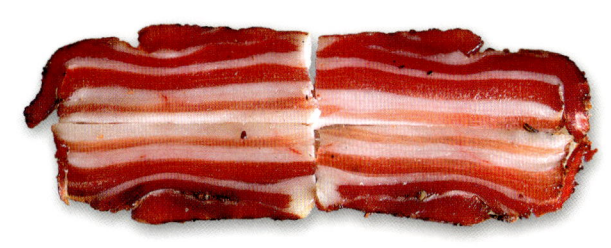

Like this bacon, many kinds of food have a conspicuous structure by nature.

Cutting a sushi roll reveals its inner structure. With many kinds of food, this effect is used for decoration.

Chapter 3: Aesthetic Appearance

The pattern of layered Damascus is similar to the wave patterns of sand found in the desert or at the beach.

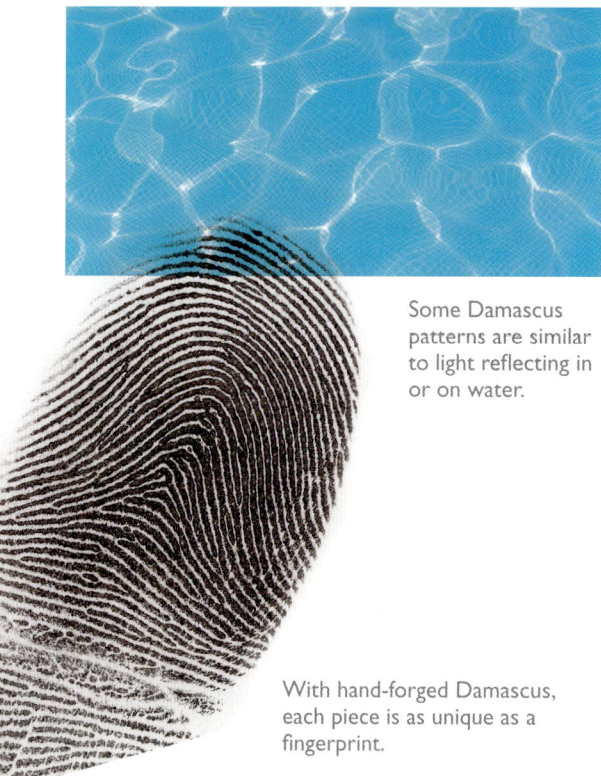

Some Damascus patterns are similar to light reflecting in or on water.

With hand-forged Damascus, each piece is as unique as a fingerprint.

3.2 Visual Parallels / Associations

Besides the parallels which are indeed based on the same principle, there are others that show a visual similarity to the patterns of Damascus. Most patterns are abstract, but nevertheless evoke various associations—surely one of the reasons for the myth of Damascus steel.

The earliest written sources that mention this material feature flowery language and allegories on the patterns—a sign that the characteristic aesthetic appearance has always inspired the human imagination. Thus, for example, around 520 A.D., the King of the Ostrogoths, Theoderic, wrote in a letter to his brother-in-law Thrasamund, king of the Vandals, the following about swords: "...you have chosen swords for us which are even capable of cutting armor, and which I praise more for their iron than for the gold they are decorated with." He also compared the pattern in the blood groove to "winding wyrm" (worms, snakes, or dragons).

In the epic Old English poem "Beowulf," written around the eighth century, there is mention of a "hard sword […] decorated with winding wyrm." The "Ekkisax" is a sword which is often mentioned in Old Nordic epic poems and described in the "Edda," which was written about 1250, as "The shield-destroyer, with gold it shines / […] On the blade there lies a blood-flecked snake / And a serpent's tail round the flat is twisted."

These examples from European culture are related to a blade structure which was common for several centuries: the so-called "wyrmfāh" blades (see 4.9.2). In sources from the Near East, other comparisons are used. The oldest known written mention of wootz steel can be found around 540 A.D., in a text by the Arabic poet Imru'ulqais, who compares the surface structure of a blade with an army of ants moving onwards. A much more recent report about this material is a Russian essay from 1814, which describes

Chapter 3: Aesthetic Appearance

the work of P. Anossov and states: "When the crucible endures even more heat, then a web-like Moiré pattern is created which slowly becomes more and more pronounced and sometimes turns into a band-like shape."

One of the initially created patterns of welded Damascus, the layered or wild Damascus (see 4.6), reminds one of waves on the surface of water because of its organic appearance, which is also the genesis of the expression "watered steel."

3.3 Design Possibilities

At first glance, the multitude of factors that influence the final aesthetic appearance of a Damascus object seem to be unmanageable. Here I will describe the theory behind these factors and how they affect the end result.

3.3.1 Color and Contrast

It may seem strange to discuss the color of Damascus steel, since it is a material which actually doesn't possess any color. It does, however, show various shades of gray which differ with respect to their luster. The spectrum ranges from a dull, dark black up to bright, silvery hues. The pattern of Damascus steel is determined by how visible the contrast between these different hues is. It is an artistic choice as to whether this contrast is striking or soft.

Because of the reflective nature of shiny metal, the presence of light plays a decisive role in the aesthetics of Damascus—objects can look quite different in various types of lighting. Also, bright areas in principle appear to be more dominant than darker ones. This should be taken into account when choosing the thickness of layers of a laminate.

The appearance of Damascus steel and the contrast of its components can be influenced by the choice of materials, and refined by the method and duration of etching. These choices are made at the very beginning of the production process and at the very end, respectively. The results produced from the available options are described in more detail in the practical component of this book.

In fact, the "colorfulness" of Damascus is quite discreet. Relying only on various shades of gray

By polishing the etched knife, the contrast in brightness is removed again. Only a slight relief structure is left. Dagger by Massimo Bernabei. *Photo: Wieland Verlag*

A marked contrast can be achieved by combining corresponding materials and etching techniques. Knife by Johannes Ebner.
Photo: Wieland Verlag

Thermal coloring enables the creation of a wide color spectrum on the Damascus surface. Bowie knife by Daniel Schärmeli. *Photo: Wieland Verlag*

Chapter 3: Aesthetic Appearance

and strong contrasts in brightness, color stays rather hidden, which draws attention to the details in the pattern.

There is one exception, however. It is possible to design a Damascus surface with color by means of various thermal processes. Hereby the material is submitted to a lengthy heat treatment, during which a layer of oxide forms on the surface of the material. The thickness of this layer is in the range of the wavelengths of visible light. Because of the interference (superposition and mutual cancellation) of specific wavelengths, the surface appears to have color. Since this effect shows up during the annealing process (after hardening and quenching), the expression "annealing colors" (tempering colors) is used here.

The same effect can be seen with oil on the surface of water and with anodized titanium. Since the layer of oxide grows at a different rates for different alloys, marked color contrasts can be created with Damascus steels. But the layer of oxide is not very resistant against mechanical loads and can easily be scratched.

3.3.2 Texture

Using a combination of prolonged acid treatment and various shades of steel can create a relief-like texture on the surface of Damascus. The individual layers, like varying elevations or little steps, can be felt when moving your finger across the surface. This effect can be enhanced further with various etching methods and repeated polishing in between. Because of the different levels of erosion, the higher- and lower-lying parts create a subtle gradient from dark and dull to bright and shiny, which looks like a cast shadow and enhances plasticity of the relief.

3.3.3 Shape and Pattern

Two basic process methods exist to give Damascus steel its final shape: stock-removal techniques (cutting, milling, grinding, etc.) and plastic deformation (forging, bending, pressing, etc.). With the first method the inner structure

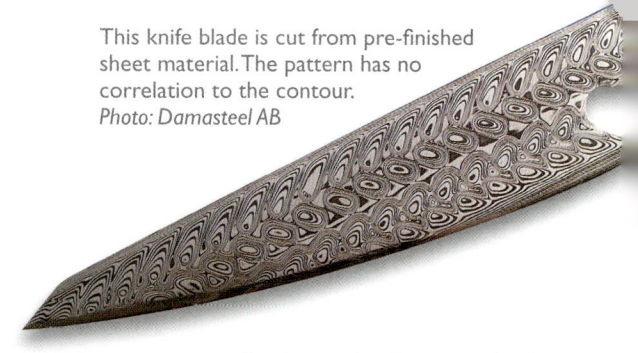

Very deep reliefs can be created with long etching times.

This knife blade is cut from pre-finished sheet material. The pattern has no correlation to the contour.
Photo: Damasteel AB

By means of several short acid baths and intermediate polishing with very fine grits, the shiny (raised) areas cast a kind of shadow.

On this axe head you can clearly see the forces employed during forging and how they changed the structure.
Photo: Damasteel AB

Chapter 3: Aesthetic Appearance

of the material isn't changed; instead, material is partially removed, which reveals another part of its surface. Plastic deformation, in contrast, affects the inner structure, which is changed together with the object as a whole.

Since the pattern of the Damascus steel is derived from its inner structure, both techniques can also be used to influence the pattern prior to the actual shaping of the object. Many pattern techniques are based on one or both of these methods. The technique of surface manipulation (see 4.6) is a good example of combining both methods.

If a previously structured flat material is contoured and shaped by means of stock-removal, the pattern ends at the borders without any relation to the shape. If the contour is mostly forged, then the pattern follows the course of the shape. It conveys an impression of the force which was applied during forging, by illustrating the deformation of the material. This method usually gives the object a more powerful appearance.

3.3.4 Combinations with other Materials and Techniques

Damascus steel is a very conspicuous material and rich in detail. Creating these details is at the center of most applications. So as not to dampen the details in Damascus, other materials and decoration techniques should only be used very cautiously. The aesthetic effect of Damascus steel can be enhanced by a selective combination with plain materials. In addition, colorful accents can be used in contrast to the original colorlessness of the material.

Conspicuously textured materials and detailed decoration techniques, like engraving, are usually in competition with the pattern of the Damascus steel. By adding these elements, the object easily looks cluttered and the observer's attention is divided. The use of such materials and techniques should be well thought out. It is very difficult to find combination techniques that are harmonious and well-balanced with Damascus steel.

Because of the many adornments, the Damascus pattern becomes part of the background. Knife by Otokar Pok.
Photo: Wieland Verlag

Here the focal point is the pattern and shape. The wooden handle accentuates the Damascus without distracting from its fineness. Knife by Jean-José Tritz.
Photo: Wieland Verlag

Chapter 4: Patterns in Damascus Steel

Patterns in Damascus Steel

The characteristic patterns of welded Damascus are created by making the inhomogeneous structure of the material visible, which is revealed on the surface of the workpiece. Through treating the workpiece with acid and polishing it to a high luster, the separate components of the material show up differently. The intensity of the contrast can be controlled through the choice of raw materials as well as the kind of surface treatment (fineness / type of polishing, duration of etching / medium for etching, etc.).

The alignment of the various materials within a workpiece, and thus the form of the pattern on the surface, is influenced by a multitude of factors (see overview to the right).

The first opportunity to make creative decisions comes when considering the alloying composition and shape of the semi-finished products from which the billet is stacked initially, as well as their order. When the source materials are put together to form a billet, they are connected by forge welding. Depending on the geometry of the source materials, two fundamental techniques for creating patterns can be distinguished: laminate (only sheet materials) and mosaic (all other combinations of semi-finished products, and perhaps also sheet materials). This way, as the name already implies, the initial, inhomogeneous material structure is created in a largely defined arrangement.

Various techniques can now be used on the resulting workpiece to influence its structure. So, for example, the number of layers of a laminate can be increased further by dividing and welding again (multiplication), or the workpiece can be turned around itself (twisting). The orientation of the structure in relation to the visual surface of the finished product is also important for creating patterns.

Finally, several independently created and treated workpieces can be combined, which rounds out the options for structure-creating techniques.

What becomes obvious here is that in the process of producing an object from Damascus steel, an almost unlimited number of influential factors exist, which all have pronounced effects on the resulting pattern. Type and order of the techniques only creates the foundation. Every single technique can also be modified by how it is executed (Is a bar twisted clockwise or counterclockwise? Or alternating? How close together should the threads be? Is the twisting done consistently or only partially?).

To not lose track of these processes when working, it is helpful to set up a plan that orders the work steps. Having experience to fall back on is also helpful. A common method for simulating the creation of complicated patterns is using modeling clay in different colors.

Since you can create as many complex patterns as you like by combining a great multitude of possibilities, a precise look at distinct steps is almost impossible. For this reason, I'd like to show some examples of patterns which illustrate the characteristic results of a certain treatment. Since some of these techniques only lead to interesting patterns in combination with others, it is not always possible to depict sample objects using the described method in a "pure form."

Chapter 4: Patterns in Damascus Steel

Factors Influencing Damascus Patterns

Source Materials

Material Composition:
Carbon Content
Manganese Content
Nickel Content

Geometry of Semi-finished Products:
Sheet Metal
Flat Section
Square Profile
Round Profile
Wire
Sphere
Tube
Mesh / Weave
Powder
Granules
Shaped Piece
Special (e.g., Chain Saw, Steel Cable)

Working Techniques

Plastic Deformation:
Forging
Cross-Sectional Deformation
Twisting
Bending
Embossing / Stamping
Rolling
Pressing

Material-removing:
Cutting
Filing
Grinding
Milling
Drilling
Turning

Surface Treatment:
Grinding
Polishing
Etching
Burnishing
Galvanizing

Techniques Creating and Influencing Structures

Techniques for Creating Structures

Laminate
Mosaic

Techniques for Influencing Structures

Orientation
Multiplication
Twisting
Surface Manipulation
Deformation
Unfolding

Combination Techniques

Cover Layer
Multiple Bars
Inlays

Chapter 4: Patterns in Damascus Steel

4.1 Laminate

Initially, and for a long time thereafter, the exclusive technique used for Damascus was the laminate. For this, sheet material is stacked and combined to form a billet. The simplest assembly is made up of alternating layers of two iron-based materials with the same thickness.

Laminates consist of layers of sheet material. With a slanted grind, the layers stand out as "contour lines."

The thickness of the layers in relation to each other create the possibility for variation. So, for example, thick, "dark" layers can be combined with thin layers of a "bright" material to create a pattern of fine, bright "veins" on a dark background. If more than two different materials are used, their order can also be varied.

On this knife by Manfred Rieger, the coarse layer structure is quite visible. Damascus by Friedrich Schneider.
Photo: Wieland Verlag

If the pattern of layers is distorted by hammer blows, so-called wild Damascus is created. Dagger by Sandor Berenyi.
Photo: Jozsef Fazekas, Jr.

Chapter 4: Patterns in Damascus Steel

4.2 Mosaics

Any arrangement of semi-finished products, except the pure layer structure of a laminate, is considered mosaic. Semi-finished products can be fashioned into a multitude of geometries. A classic method is the use of bars with a square cross-section, but there are no limits to one's imagination. A mosaic, for example, can also be assembled from wires, tubes, spheres, powder, mesh/weave, various prismatic semi-finished products, or even from pieces with custom-made pieces. In addition to the bitmap mosaic, I will also introduce the following variations in more detail: spirograph mosaic, matrix mosaic, jigsaw mosaic, and mosaics from finished parts.

With many mosaic techniques, the pattern will only show up on the front sides of the bar after welding. This kind of construction is called "end grain pattern Damascus." To make this pattern visible on the longitudinal surface (which for a knife is the surface you look on), further processes are necessary: for example, twisting (see 4.5) or unfolding (4.8).

4.2.1 Bitmap Mosaic

A very basic method is the assembly of a billet from bars with square cross sections. By positioning the materials appropriately, one can create a chess board, a simple pictograph, or even an inscription. For this, the same rules apply as for a digital bitmap graphic: a raster of square "pixels," which can either be black or white, are arranged in a pattern. In the case of Damascus steel, the black and white are variations in metallic luster. To set accents, the square bars are often framed or divided by sheet material or laminate billets.

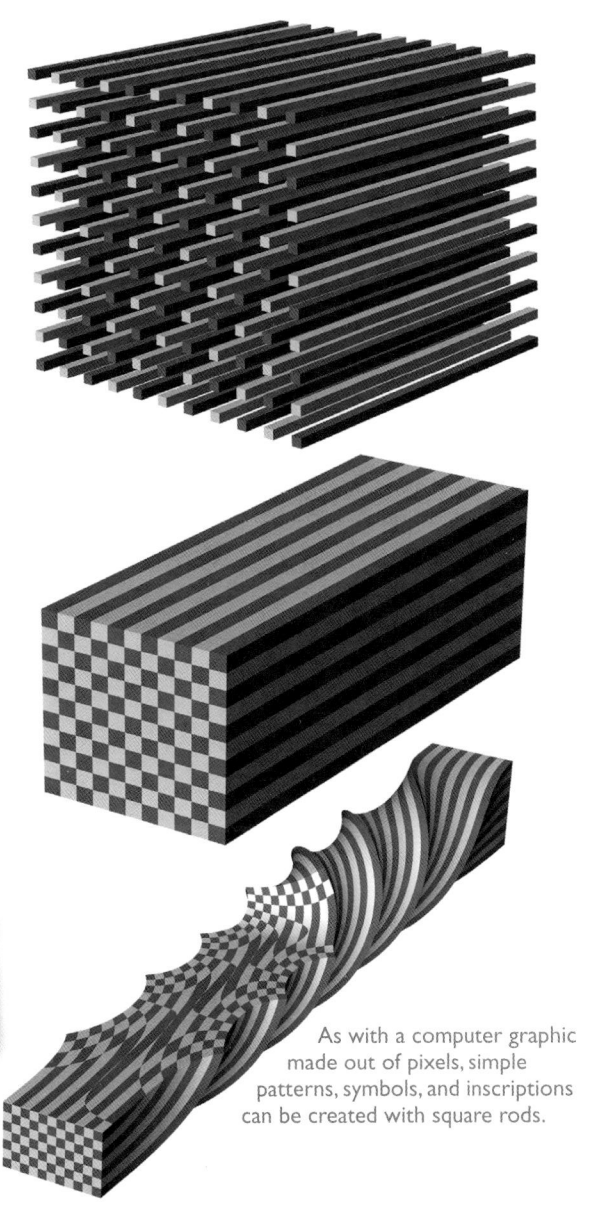

Inscription Damascus by Mick Maxen. The letters were made visible on the longitudinal side of the bar by twisting. *Photo: Mick Maxen*

As with a computer graphic made out of pixels, simple patterns, symbols, and inscriptions can be created with square rods.

Chapter 4: Patterns in Damascus Steel

4.2.2 Spirograph Mosaic

This variation has a purely orthogonal structure, similar to that of the bitmap mosaic. For this, square bars are used, which are all made from the same steel; these are then divided by thin sheets of another material. The bright lines are thus arranged like the lines of graph paper.

Quite often this mosaic is also further structured by means of surface manipulation (see 4.6). Thus filigree patterns of parallel lines and lines crossing each other are created, which sometimes look like the drawings of a spirograph.

Knife by André Thorburn with a blade of superficially shaped spirograph Damascus by Ettore Gianferrari.
Photo: Wieland Verlag

The blade on this knife by George Bartman is made from several stripes of twisted spirograph Damascus.
Photo: Wieland Verlag

Thin sheets of metal stand out as fine, intersecting lines on the spirograph Damascus.

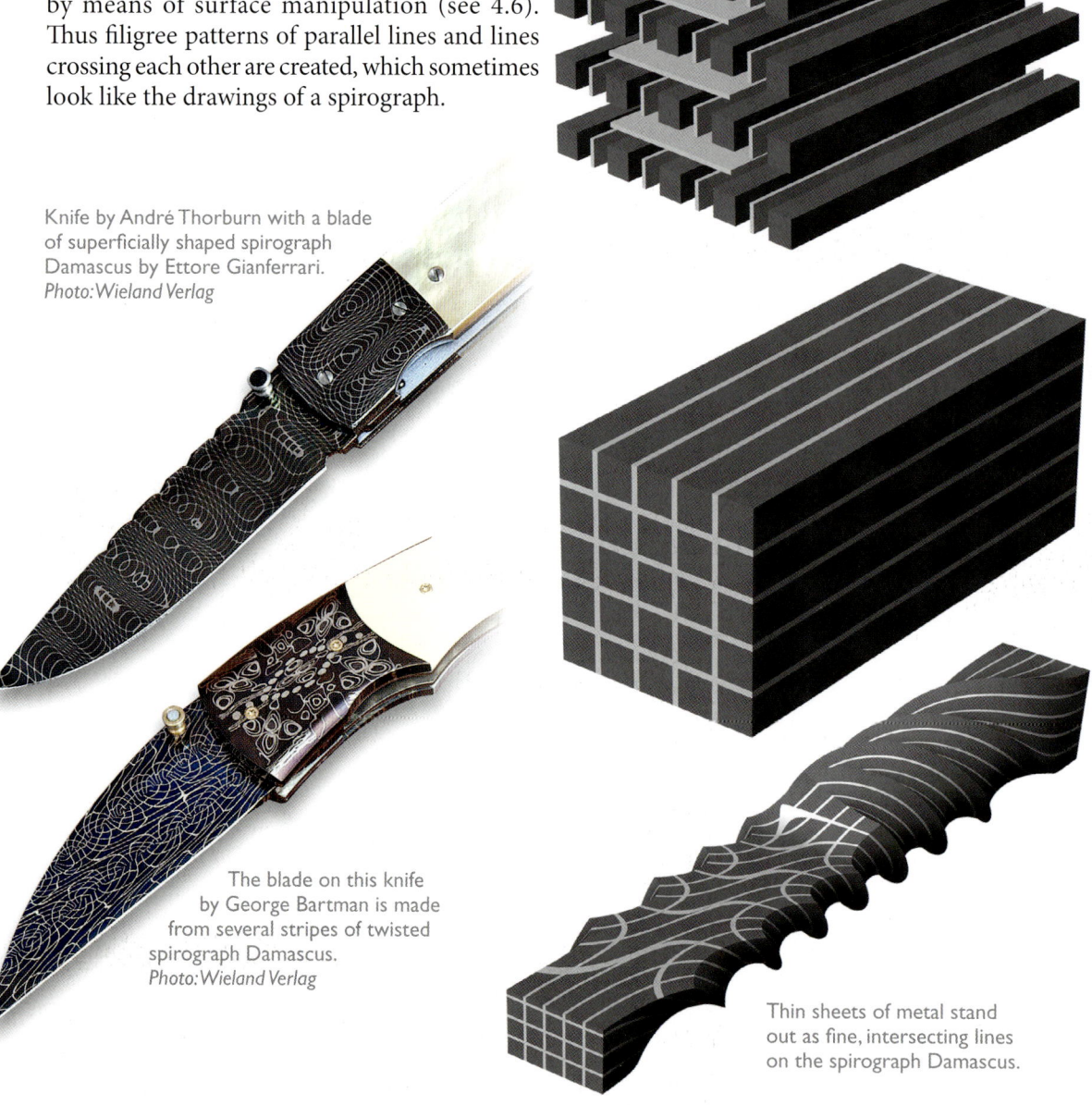

Chapter 4: Patterns in Damascus Steel

4.2.3 Matrix Mosaic

For this method, wires or other parts are embedded into a matrix of flat materials and then welded together. Here, the continuous layers usually are made from the same material, while the parts of the incomplete layers are made from one or more different raw materials. Depending on the kind of arrangement and the shape of the embedded parts as well as the orientation of the layers with respect to the visual surface, the resulting patterns can vary greatly.

With matrix mosaic, wires or other small parts are embedded between continuous layers.

Bowl of matrix mosaic by Gunther Löbach.

Chapter 4: Patterns in Damascus Steel

4.2.4 Jigsaw Mosaic

The classic method for creating ornaments, pictures, and inscriptions can be refined immensely with the help of modern, computerized production processes. Laser and water jet cutting, but especially electric discharge machining (EDM, sometimes also called spark erosion) allow the production of profiles with all kinds of imaginable contours in the cross-section. Besides that, it is possible to produce positive and negative structures from different materials and to put them together like pieces of a jigsaw puzzle. Another method is the use of such a positive while the negative space (in a surrounding metal box) is filled up with powder or granules.

The blade of this knife made by Pierre Reverdy consists of several bars of twisted jigsaw mosaic with a rose pattern.
Photo: German Blade Museum, Solingen, Lutz Hoffmeister

Parts with diverse shapes are produced as positive and negative structures from different steel types and put together.

With the jigsaw mosaic technique any "image" can be produced. Knife by Pavel Sevecek.
Photo: Wieland Verlag

Chapter 4: Patterns in Damascus Steel

4.2.5 Mosaic from Finished Parts

Here, finished parts made from individual steel components are fused to form a solid block. An often-used variation of this pattern is made from the chains of chain saws, but motorcycle and bicycle chains are also suitable. The different components of a chain saw (chain links, bolts, and, on occasion, also saw teeth) are made from different steel types, depending on their individual requirements. The chain is folded together, heated up, compressed like a sponge until a billet is created which is as free from pores as possible, then it is finally forge welded. Depending on the work method, the pattern of the chain links can either be preserved almost completely or lengthened and totally changed by drawing out and folding. The manner in which the chain is folded has great influence on the resulting patterns, too. Steel cables can also be welded into a compact rod. The resulting pattern consists of characteristic spots—in principle, the wire is a twisted mosaic rod with very wide pitch. Although the individual wires of the cable are made of the same material, the border areas show a filigree pattern. A strong contrast can't be achieved this way.

A steel cable, in principle, is a twisted mosaic rod. Because of the identical steel types, the achievable contrast is weak. Only the welds can be seen. Knife by Christian Deminie.
Photo: Christian Deminie

With careful treatment, the pattern of the chain saw chain is still quite visible after welding.

Chain knife made by Martin Steinhorst.
Photo: Martin Steinhorst

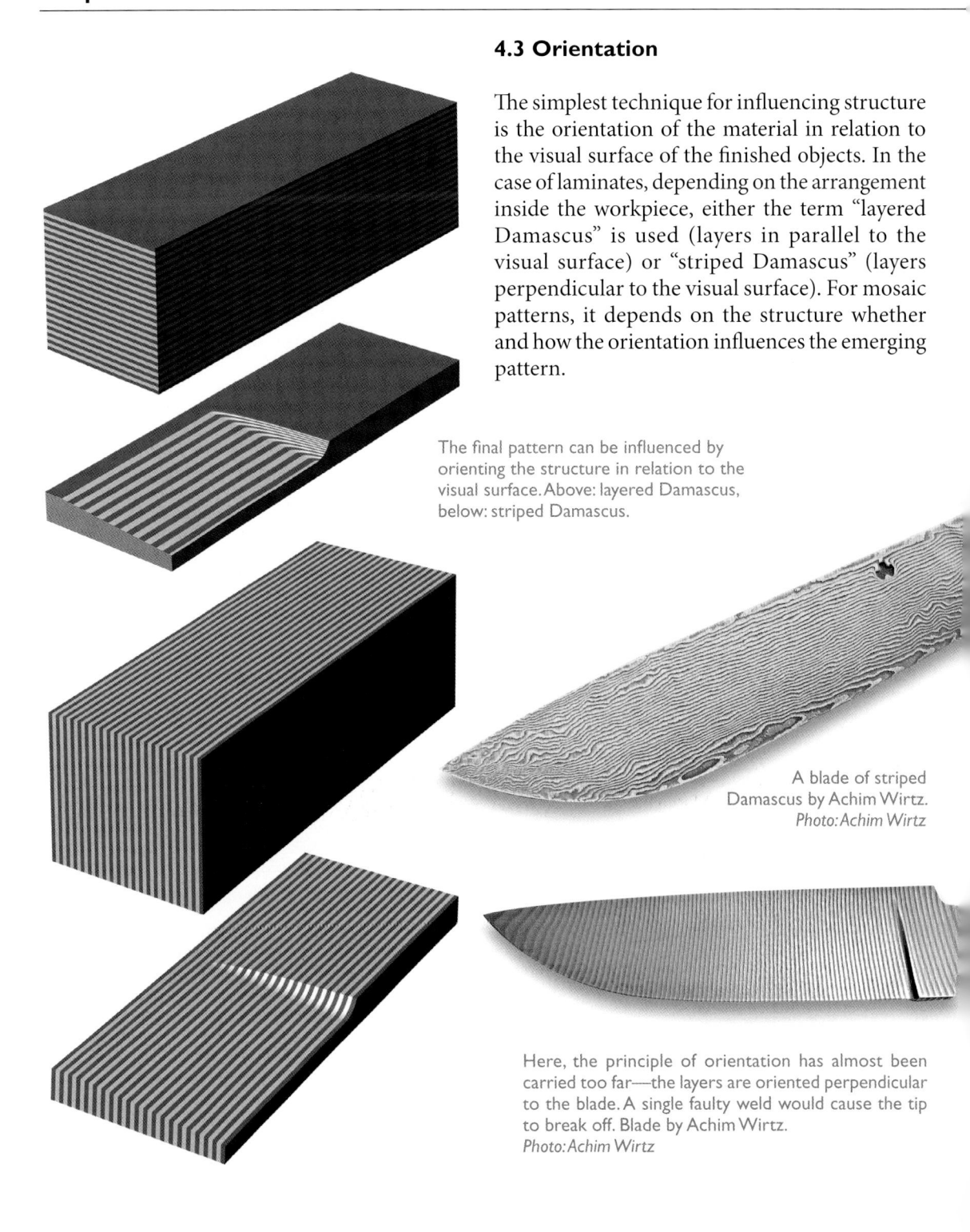

Chapter 4: Patterns in Damascus Steel

4.3 Orientation

The simplest technique for influencing structure is the orientation of the material in relation to the visual surface of the finished objects. In the case of laminates, depending on the arrangement inside the workpiece, either the term "layered Damascus" is used (layers in parallel to the visual surface) or "striped Damascus" (layers perpendicular to the visual surface). For mosaic patterns, it depends on the structure whether and how the orientation influences the emerging pattern.

The final pattern can be influenced by orienting the structure in relation to the visual surface. Above: layered Damascus, below: striped Damascus.

A blade of striped Damascus by Achim Wirtz.
Photo: Achim Wirtz

Here, the principle of orientation has almost been carried too far—the layers are oriented perpendicular to the blade. A single faulty weld would cause the tip to break off. Blade by Achim Wirtz.
Photo: Achim Wirtz

Chapter 4: Patterns in Damascus Steel

4.4 Multiplication

This is a very basic technique, which overlaps with the structure-creating techniques. Hereby the workpiece is divided into two or more parts which again are put together and welded into a single billet. Increasing the number of layers of a laminate is the most common use of multiplication. If a laminate billet is divided in the center and folded, the number of layers is doubled—if the billet is cut into more parts, this effect is heightened even more. Because of

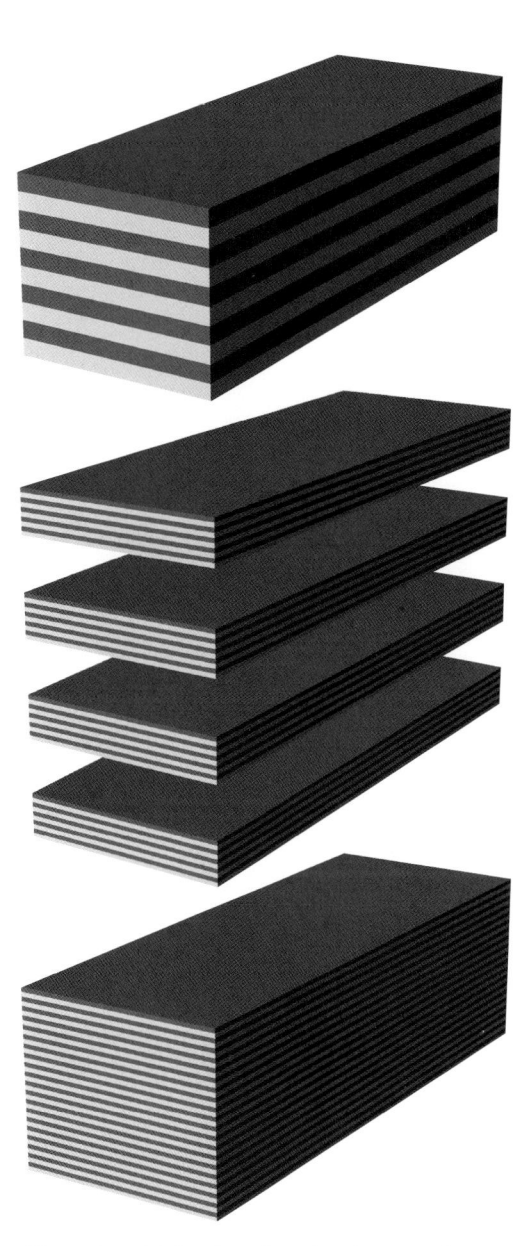

Through multiplication of an already created Damascus structure, the pattern becomes finer.

Mosaic can also be multiplied. But here you should always work in only two directions to avoid distorting the pattern.

Chapter 4: Patterns in Damascus Steel

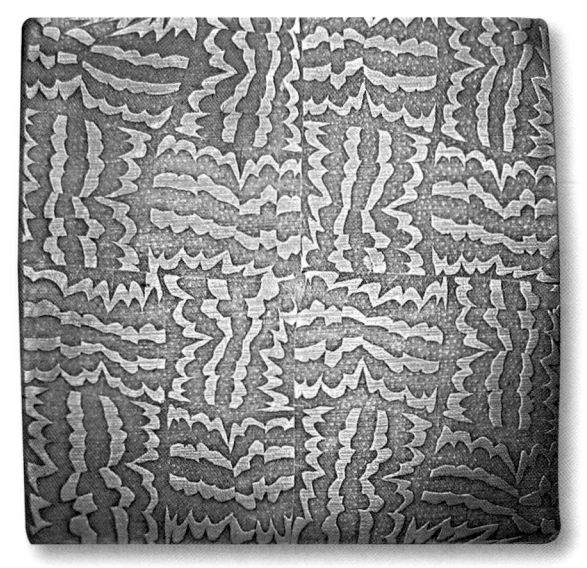

the exponential increase, a few welds can thus create a very high number of layers. But practice shows layers that are too fine are not favorable for creating patterns because the eye can barely distinguish the individual layers anymore.

Another possibility for varying the multiplication is the orientation (see 4.3) of the parts with respect to each other. Laminate billets, for example, can be arranged at an angle of 90° to each other (basket weave pattern).

With respect to the multiplication of mosaics, basically the same rules apply, but as an additional factor it is also possible to turn the pieces around lengthwise and to thus create a mirror image composition.

If square rods are rotated 90° to each other during multiplication, a basket weave pattern is created. Mosaic by Achim Wirtz.
Photo: Achim Wirtz

Fine laminate construction with 96 layers. Modified Opinel by Gunther Löbach.

In contrast, a laminate with coarse structure (9 layers). Modified Opinel by Gunther Löbach.

Chapter 4: Patterns in Damascus Steel

4.5 Twisting

For this technique, a prepared bar of laminate or mosaic Damascus is twisted: i.e., turned around itself. This way right-handed or left-handed bars can be created. Also influential for the emerging pattern is how tight the bar is twisted (pitch) and what kind of cross-section it had prior to twisting (square, octagon, circle, etc.). Besides this, a bar can also be only partially twisted or alternately, twisted in the opposite direction. The wave-like pattern of a bar twisted with alternating direction is called "maidenhair Damascus."

Often several twisted bars are bundled together and welded again. Combining left- and right-handed bars creates a symmetrical pattern. Depending on how much material is ground off a twisted bar, very different patterns emerge. This is caused by the position of the layers, which steadily changes over the length of the workpiece.

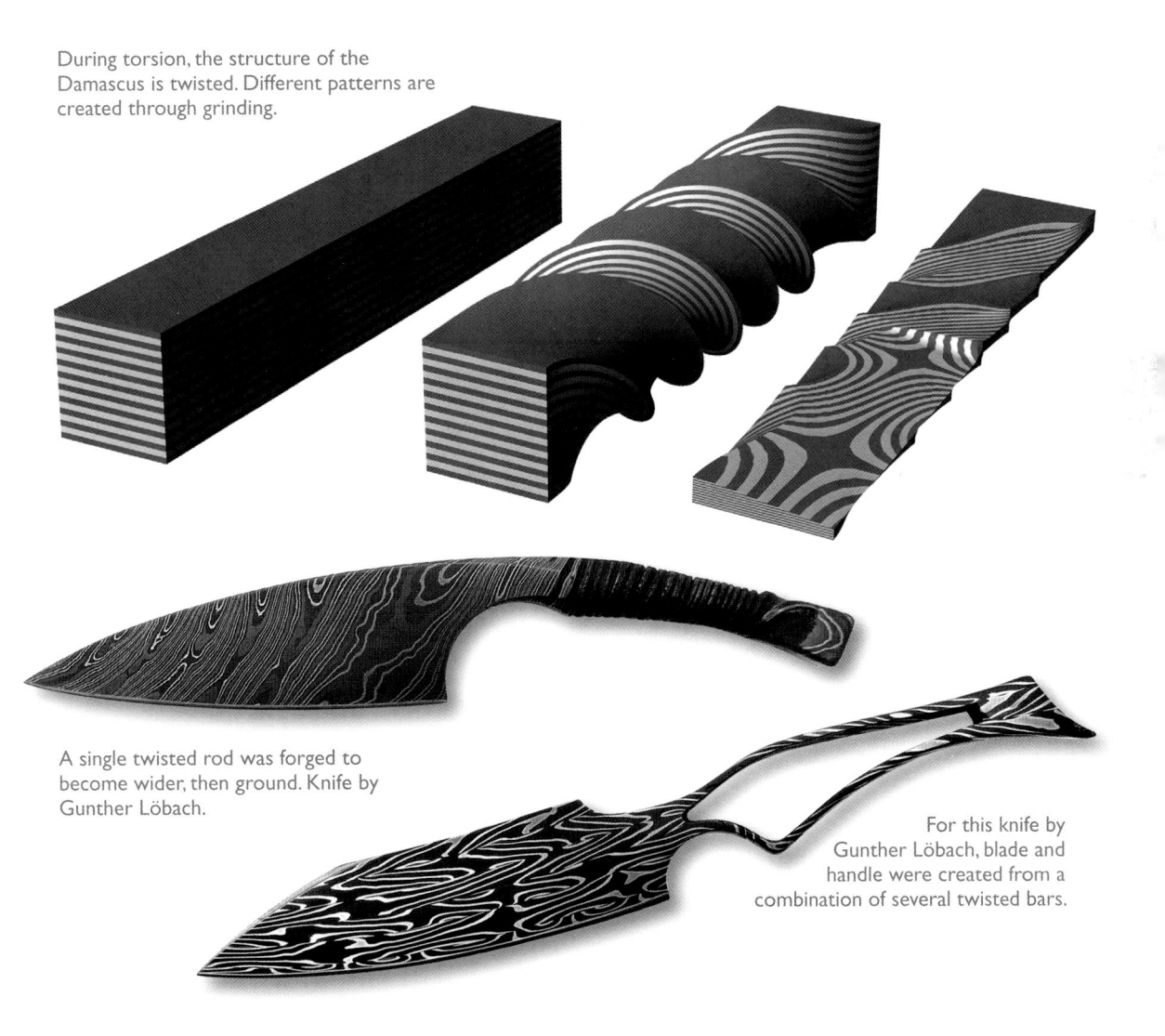

During torsion, the structure of the Damascus is twisted. Different patterns are created through grinding.

A single twisted rod was forged to become wider, then ground. Knife by Gunther Löbach.

For this knife by Gunther Löbach, blade and handle were created from a combination of several twisted bars.

55

Chapter 4: Patterns in Damascus Steel

4.5.1 Combining Several Twisted Bars

In anticipation of chapter 4.9 and the multiple bar techniques described there, I want to separately introduce the combination of several twisted bars here because, to a large extent, they are common. Consistently twisted and/or alternately twisted bars are hereby forged or ground to create a square cross-section. The bars then are put in parallel to form a flat billet and are subsequently welded together. To create a consistent pattern, the pitch must be identical for all bars. One must also take into account that the bars are growing in length and the pitch is enlarged during welding and forging.

A variation is the use of uneven or only partially twisted bars. The lengthwise arrangement leads to even more possible variations.

4.5.2 Phases of Grinding

Since the structure inside a twisted bar is distorted, at some points the layers are parallel to the surface and at others they are perpendicular to it. When grinding the surface, first some diagonal lines show up tilted at the same angle, which is given by the pitch of the torsion. If more material is removed, the pattern starts to adjust to a tangent graph, which is also based on a circular "movement." The more you grind towards the center of the bar, the more the curves move into each other, until finally a star-shaped pattern emerges.

By combining several bars, alternately twisted to the left and right at the same pitch, a uniform pattern is created. Demonstration piece and blade by Peter J. Stienen. *Photo: Peter. J. Stienen*

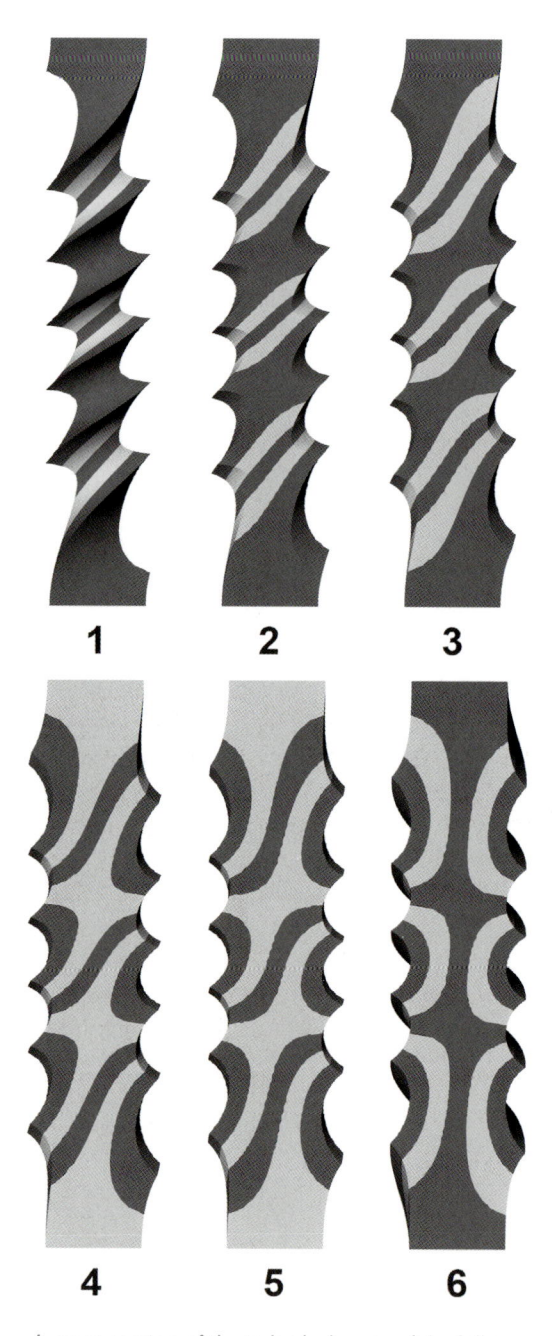

A cross section of the individual parts of the billet.

Chapter 4: Patterns in Damascus Steel

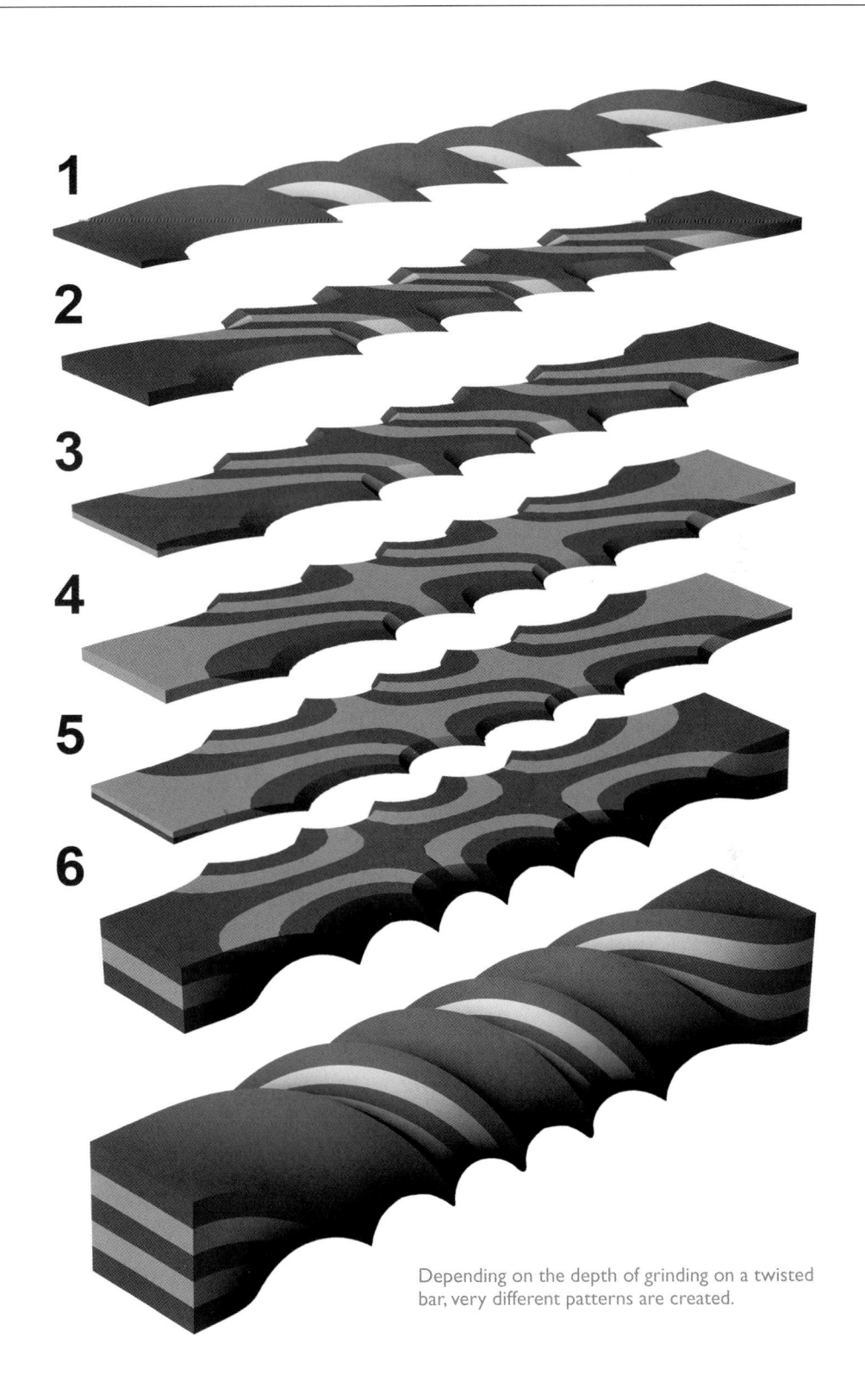

Depending on the depth of grinding on a twisted bar, very different patterns are created.

Chapter 4: Patterns in Damascus Steel

4.6 Surface Manipulation

For this group of patterns, the source material is usually a relatively fine laminate. The basic principle for surface manipulation is the partial removal of material so that the layer structure in this area is cut open and the pattern is revealed. To achieve this, either material is taken off in some places first and then the surface is equalized again by deformation, or the sequence is reversed. This means that first the surface is shaped, then ground flat or milled. A series of "classic" patterns exist which are created by surface manipulation. The nomenclature for most of them is inconsistent.

4.6.1 Embossing Technique

With this method of surface manipulation, the workpiece (usually a laminate billet) is deformed first. This can be done by forging it with the hammer peen, embossing with suitable punches, flattening hammers, profiled rolls, or with forging dies. During the next process, the elevated parts are removed by means of grinding or milling, until a flat surface has again been achieved. Hereby, the layers of the embossed pattern are revealed and the pattern is thus depicted on the surface.

4.6.2 Notching Technique

Contrary to the embossing technique, here the work steps are taken in reverse order. As before, the source material usually is a laminate billet. During the first step a relief is created by removing material. Common methods are filing, milling, drilling, or grinding. The layers in the treated areas are revealed in this way. Finally, the workpiece is flattened again by deformation (forging or rolling), which means the layers are deformed and thus, too, create patterns on the surface. With respect to the notching technique it has to be taken into account that the workpiece is drawn out (lengthened) during forging or rolling and hence the pattern is distorted accordingly.

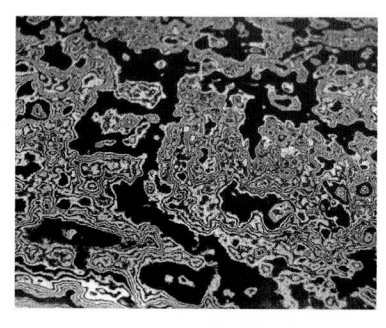

"Wild Damascus" a surface manipulation pattern created by "random" deformation or notching of the workpiece. Blade by Peter J. Stienen. *Photo: Peter J. Stienen*

"Large Roses" a surface manipulation pattern. Blade by Peter J. Stienen. *Photo: Peter J. Stienen*

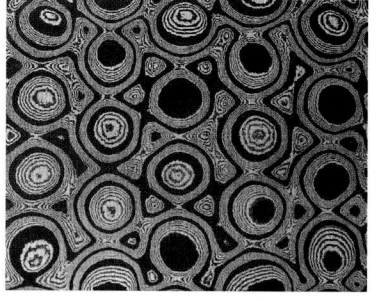

"Small Roses" surface manipulation pattern. Blade by Peter J. Stienen. *Photo: Peter J. Stienen*

"Ladder" surface manipulation pattern. Blade by Peter J. Stienen. *Photo: Peter J. Stienen*

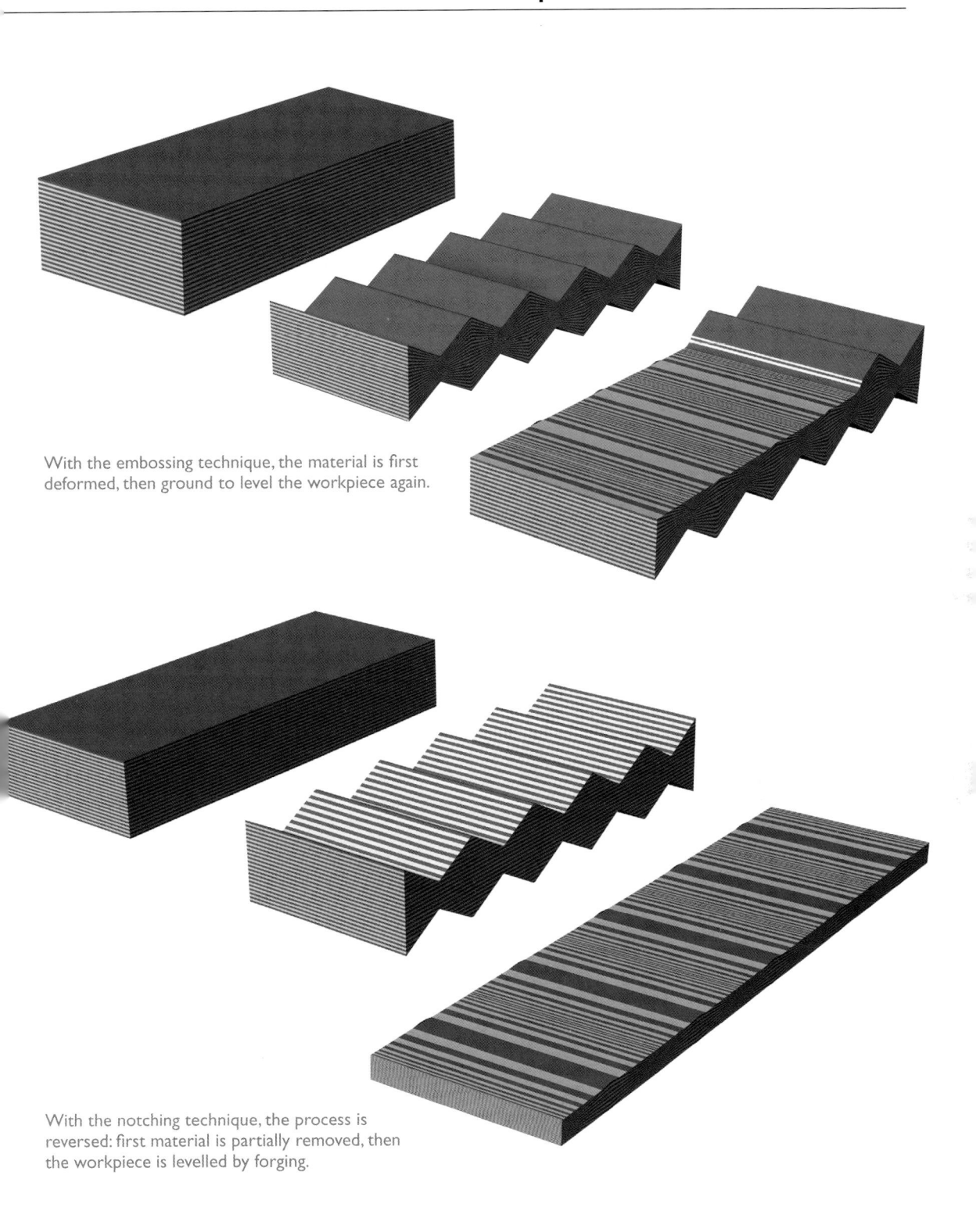

Chapter 4: Patterns in Damascus Steel

With the embossing technique, the material is first deformed, then ground to level the workpiece again.

With the notching technique, the process is reversed: first material is partially removed, then the workpiece is levelled by forging.

Chapter 4: Patterns in Damascus Steel

4.7 Deformation

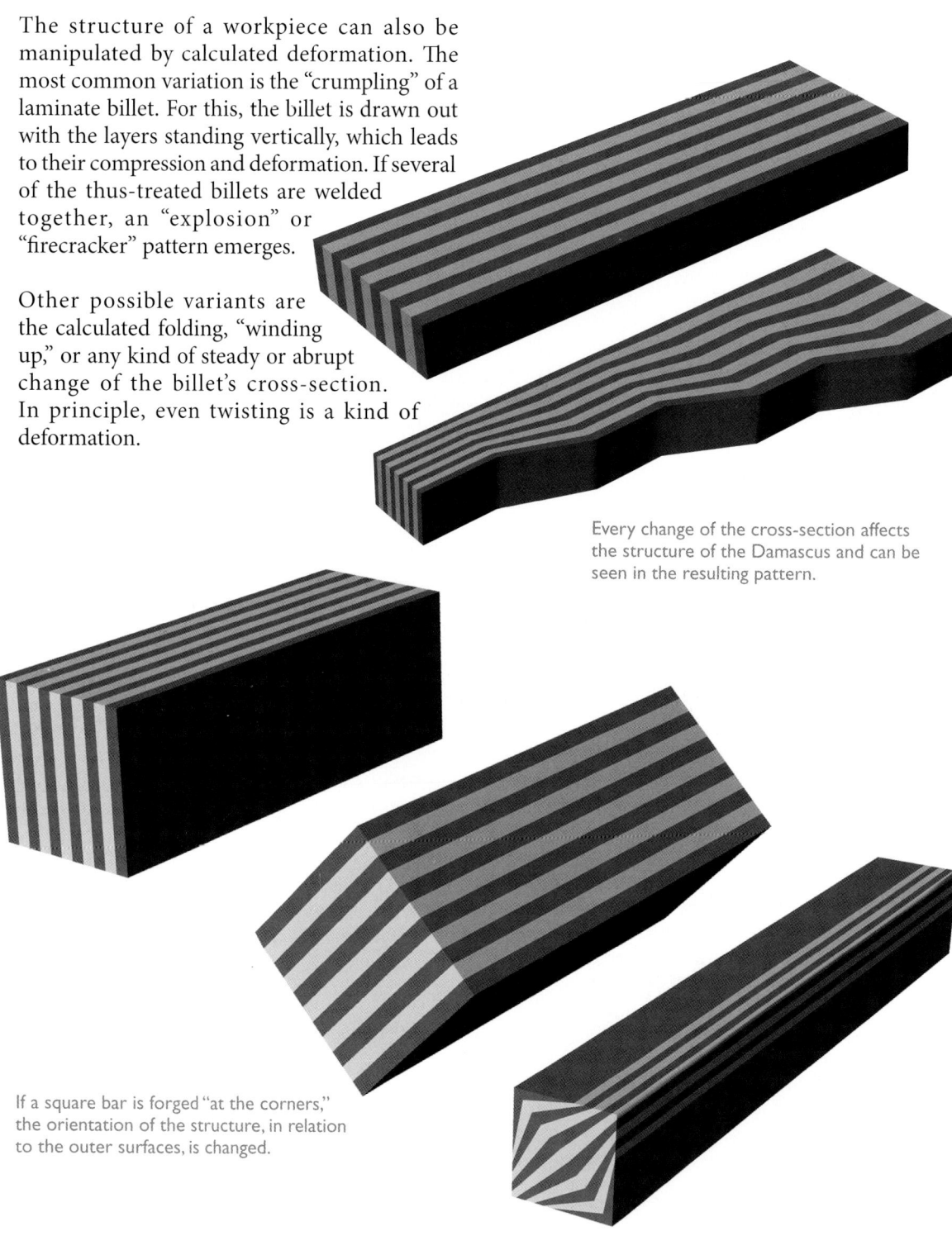

The structure of a workpiece can also be manipulated by calculated deformation. The most common variation is the "crumpling" of a laminate billet. For this, the billet is drawn out with the layers standing vertically, which leads to their compression and deformation. If several of the thus-treated billets are welded together, an "explosion" or "firecracker" pattern emerges.

Other possible variants are the calculated folding, "winding up," or any kind of steady or abrupt change of the billet's cross-section. In principle, even twisting is a kind of deformation.

Every change of the cross-section affects the structure of the Damascus and can be seen in the resulting pattern.

If a square bar is forged "at the corners," the orientation of the structure, in relation to the outer surfaces, is changed.

Chapter 4: Patterns in Damascus Steel

4.8 Unfolding

To reveal the pattern on the front side of a billet (end grain Damascus, see 4.2), the bar can be cut into slices, which in turn can be welded against each other and/or be welded as a cover layer (see 4.9), like tiles on top of a continuous layer. To simplify this principle, the mosaic bar can also be cut from alternating sides and unfolded like an accordion. This creates a mirror-imaged series of the front-side pattern (similar to bookmatching wood veneers), which opens up interesting possibilities.

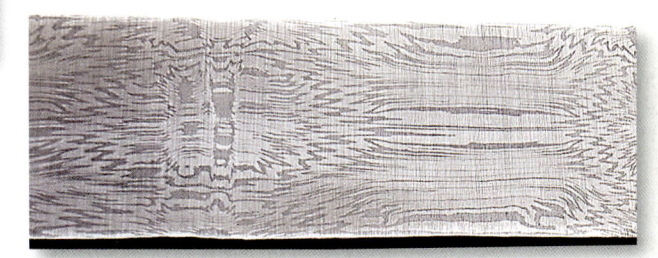

This mosaic by Achim Wirtz was put together from various deformed Damascus rods.
Photo: Achim Wirtz

The drawn-out areas of the pattern, which are created at the unfolded bottom area of the notches, are quite visible. Unfolded explosion pattern Damascus by Achim Wirtz.
Photo: Achim Wirtz

Another mosaic variant by Achim Wirtz combining various deformation techniques.
Photo: Achim Wirtz

Knife by Achim Wirtz with a blade of unfolded explosion pattern Damascus.
Photo: Achim Wirtz

Chapter 4: Patterns in Damascus Steel

To "unreel" the end grain pattern of a Damascus billet so it is visible on the longitudinal side, the bar can be notched on both sides alternately and unfolded like an accordion.

Chapter 4: Patterns in Damascus Steel

4.9 Cover Layer / Multiple Bars

Many of the complicated Damascus patterns are assembled from different components. In principle, this is, once again, a structure-creating technique for which several, independently reworked structures can be combined. With respect to the orientation of the Damascus components, these combinations can be divided into two groups: a laminar arrangement is called a cover layer technique. Here the contact areas of the components are oriented parallel to the visual surface, similar to layered Damascus. If the contact areas are perpendicular to the visual surface, as with striped Damascus, the result is called multiple bar technique. There are also hybrids of both techniques.

The already great variety of patterns can be extended infinitely this way. The following examples represent some of the possibilities of this vast group.

Multiple bar blade by Achim Wirtz from differently twisted mosaic rods and intermediate layers.
Photo: Achim Wirtz

Knife by Norbert Leitner with cover layer blade. Damascus by Peter J. Stienen.
Photo: Peter J. Stienen

Cover layer blade with coarse layer structure by Thomas Hauschild.
Photo: Wieland Verlag

Bowie knife by Achim Wirtz with multiple bar technique. Coarsely and finely twisted rods were combined (with intermediate layers) to form a blade.
Photo: Achim Wirtz

Chapter 4: Patterns in Damascus Steel

4.9.1 Composite Blades

Very early in the history of Damascus steel, combinations were already in use. A typical example is composite blades. Even among the oldest Damascus finds, the blades featured very complex structures. The combination of different materials and/or patterned bars was most probably used for decorative purposes as well as to enhance the technical qualities and to save material, which took a great deal of effort to produce. So, for creating patterns on sword blades, quite often twisted bars in the center were framed by welded-on (soled-on) cutting areas of layered or striped Damascus (multiple bar technique).

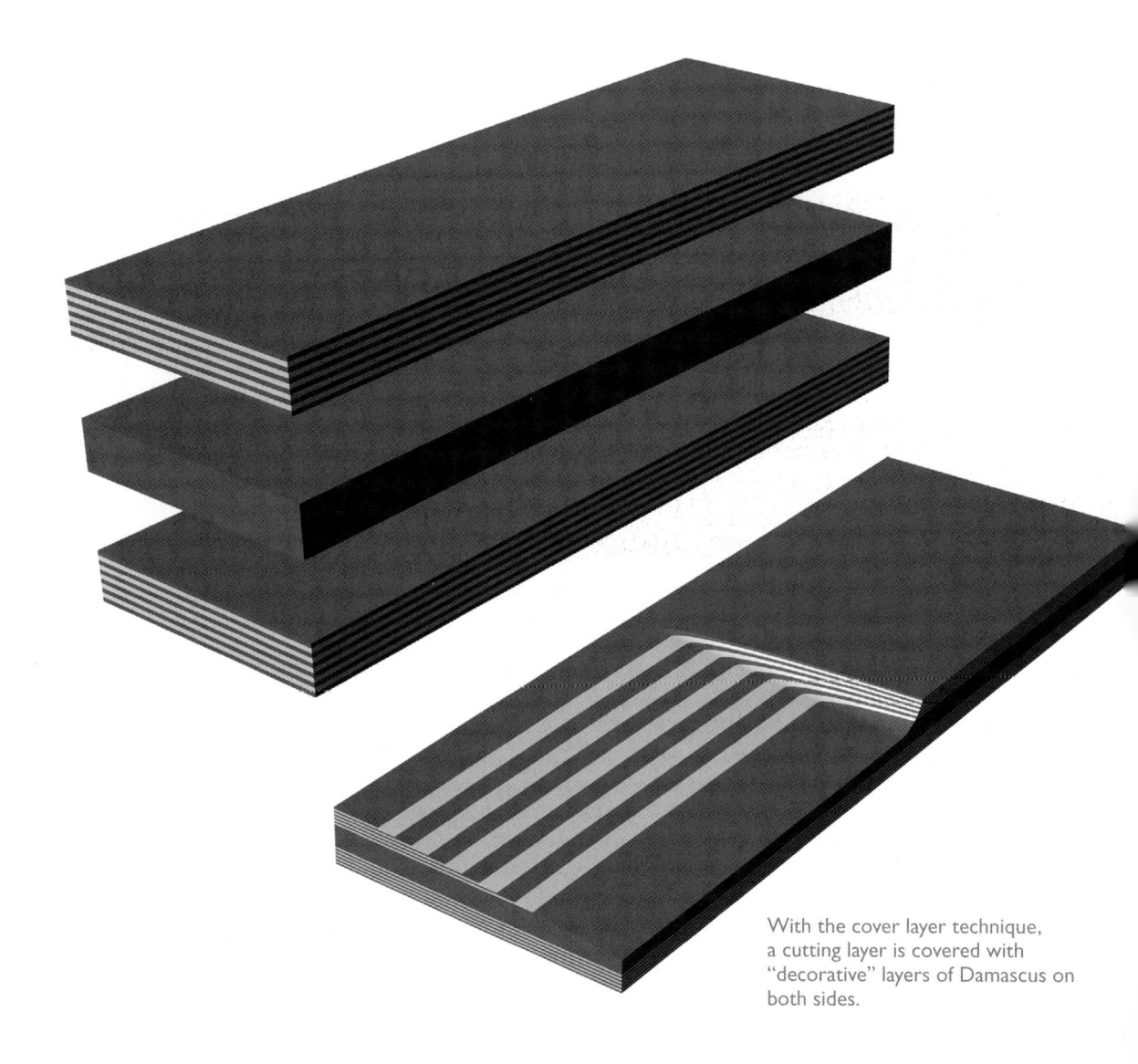

With the cover layer technique, a cutting layer is covered with "decorative" layers of Damascus on both sides.

Chapter 4: Patterns in Damascus Steel

With respect to the cover layer technique, there exist two basic variants: for the first one, a bar of soft iron is used in the center of the blade, which is surrounded on all sides by hardenable material. For the second variant, a hardenable cutting layer is plated on both sides with "decor layers" of soft material. This procedure is similar to veneering some cheap wood with thin layers of high-quality material. On the one hand, the elasticity of the blade is enhanced by this macroscopic composite structure; on the other hand, less of the expensive-to-produce Damascus is used.

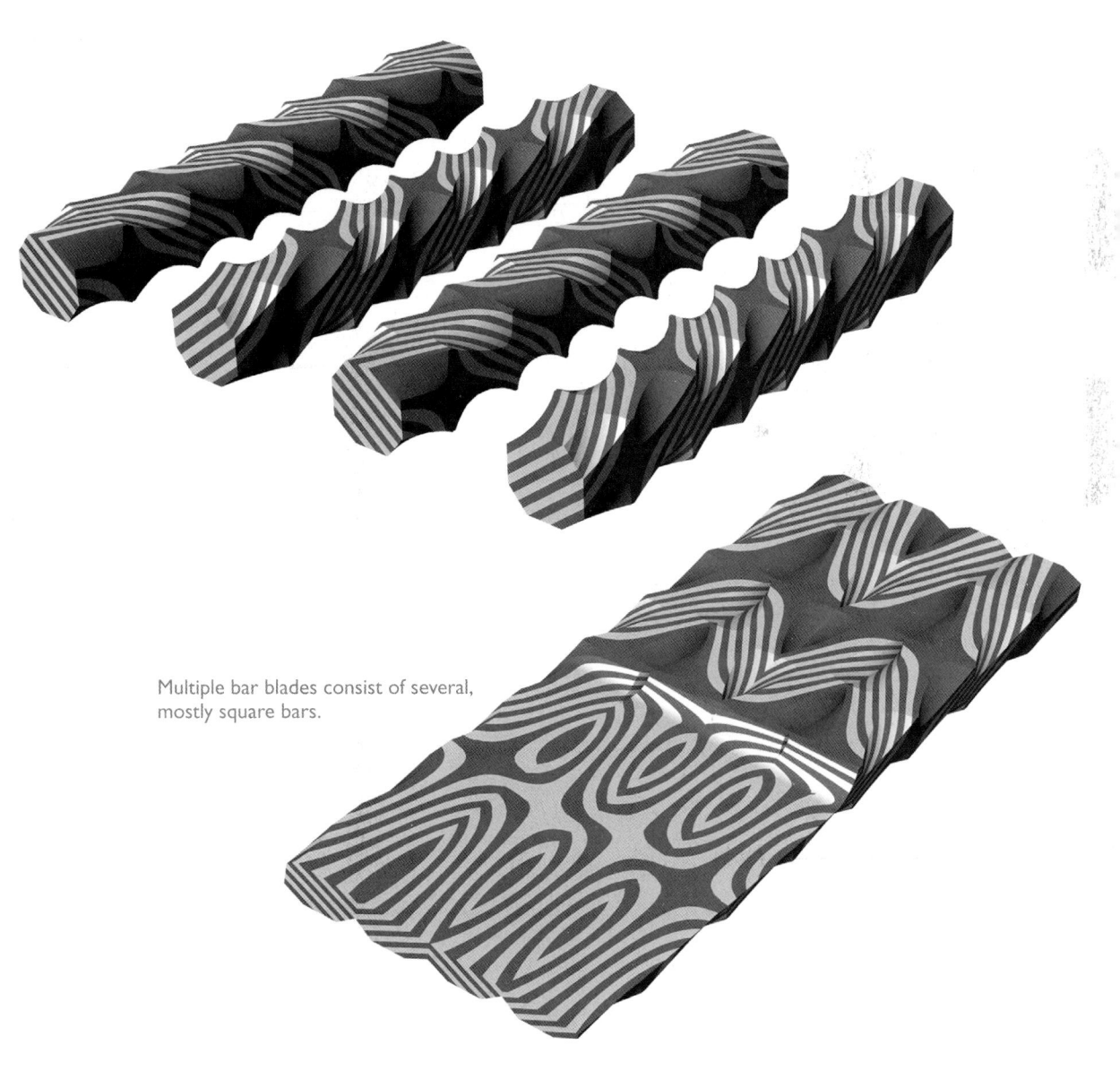

Multiple bar blades consist of several, mostly square bars.

Chapter 4: Patterns in Damascus Steel

4.9.2 "Wyrmfāh" Damascus

The expression "wyrmfāh" is used for composite blades with a blade core of several twisted bars, to which cutting areas from layered Damascus were fused on both sides. The term is based on various historical sources in which the pattern of the blades is described. This specific blade composition was often used conspicuously and thus it established its own name. One of the best-preserved and most well-known examples of this blade type is the Sutton-Hoo broad sword, named after the location of its find, an Anglo-Saxon ship-burial on the east coast of England.

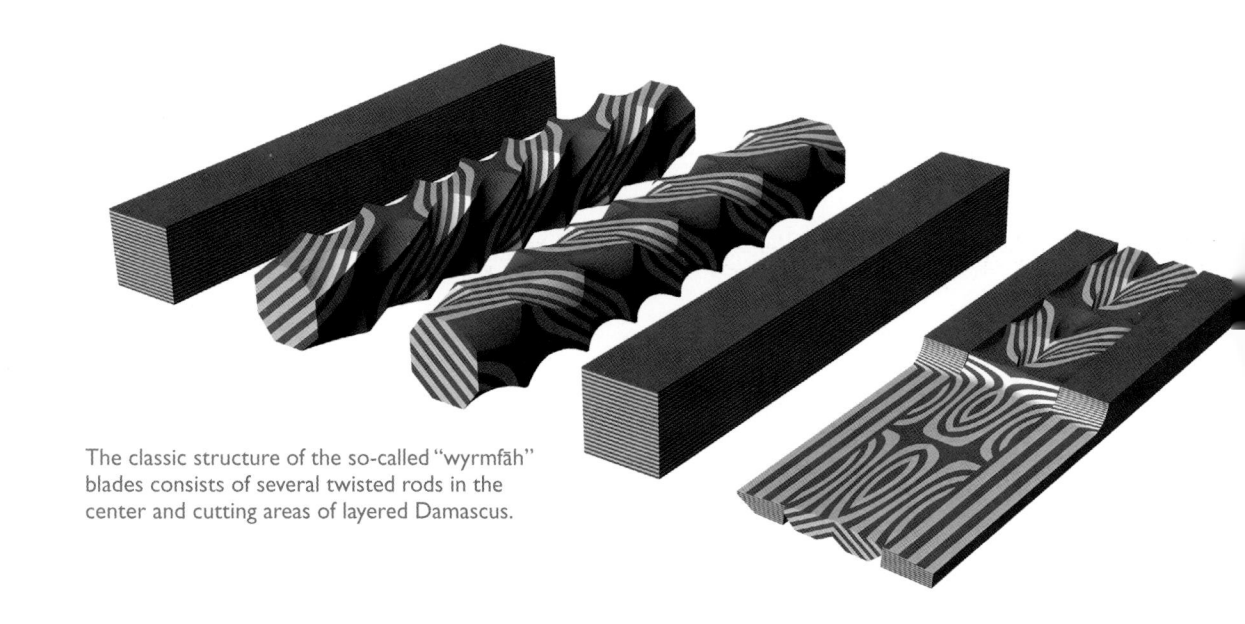

The classic structure of the so-called "wyrmfāh" blades consists of several twisted rods in the center and cutting areas of layered Damascus.

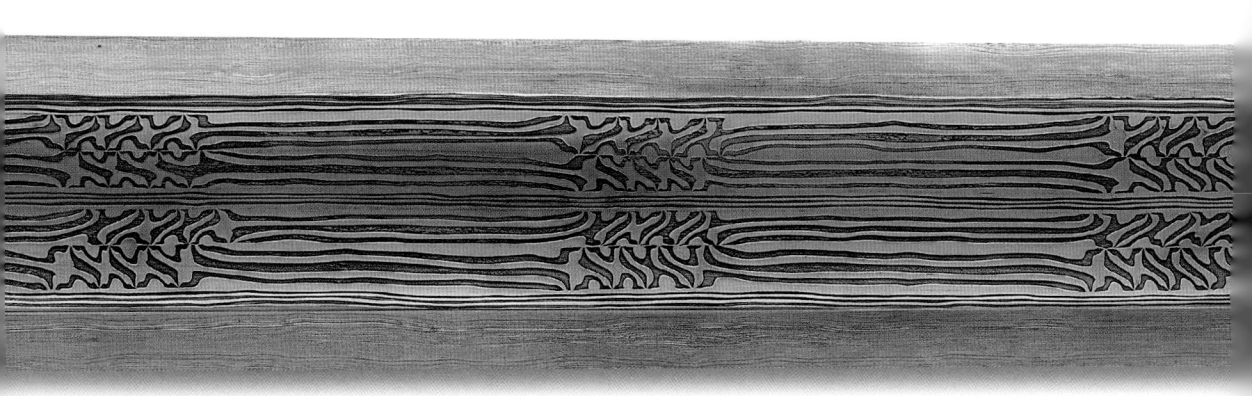

Reconstructed blade of the Sutton-Hoo broad sword by Markus Balbach with "wyrmfāh" structure.
Photo: German Blade Museum, Solingen, Lutz Hoffmeister

Chapter 4: Patterns in Damascus Steel

4.10 Inlays

Another possibility for combining different Damascus structures is the inlay technique. Here, a slice of a previously produced end-grain Damascus (usually a mosaic) is inserted into the surface of the workpiece. For this, a depression is prepared (i.e., by milling or stamping) into which the inlay is fitted. Finally, the parts are connected by means of forge welding.

A special version of the inlay technique is the so called "wire damascening." For this technique a wire is inlaid into a prepared groove of the workpiece, then forge welded. The wire is made from a different steel type than the grooved object. It can also be made from strands of different steels, which may be twisted to form a steel cable or braided like a plait.

With the inlay technique, slices of a mosaic rod (often a jigsaw mosaic) are inlaid into a basic material.

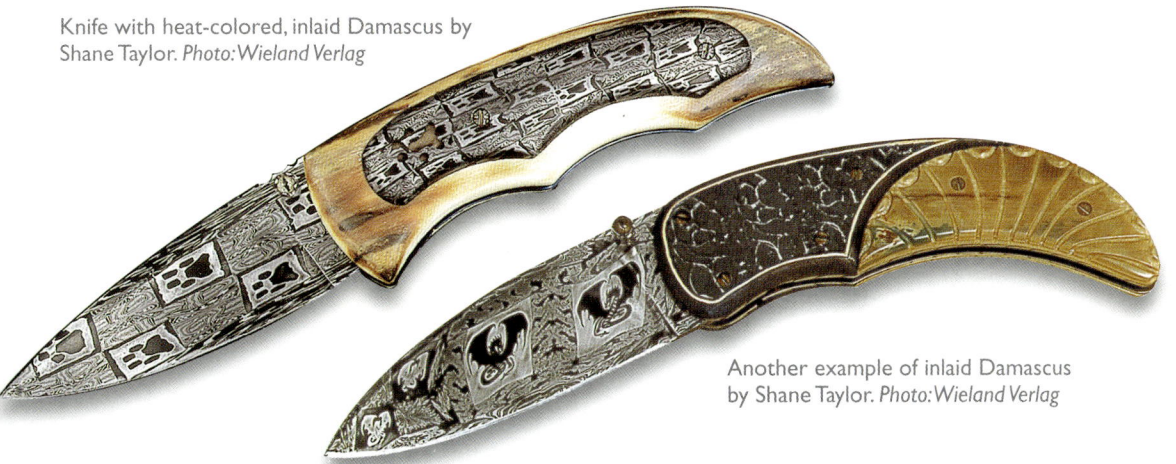

Knife with heat-colored, inlaid Damascus by Shane Taylor. *Photo: Wieland Verlag*

Another example of inlaid Damascus by Shane Taylor. *Photo: Wieland Verlag*

Chapter 4: Patterns in Damascus Steel

4.11 Gallery of Damascus Steel Art

The objects in this gallery show a small selection of how diverse Damascus steel can look as well as the variety of its uses.

"Cutting egg" by Martin Steinhorst. Smelted steel, carburized. Deconstructed knife design: "What can be omitted with a knife?"
Photo: Martin Steinhorst

Chapter 4: Patterns in Damascus Steel

Rings of layered Damascus by Aliki Apoussidou.
Photo: Aliki Apoussidou

Three rings by Martin Steinhorst. Damascus steel forged out of one piece, coarsely ground, left raw: "Forging surface—what is underneath?"
Photo: Martin Steinhorst

Chapter 4: Patterns in Damascus Steel

Pendant by Mick Maxen. Twisted Damascus from C70 and 15N20 (blued), framed by white gold.
Photo: Mick Maxen

Jewel box by Mick Maxen. Put together from seven Damascus rods (C70 / 15N20), some of which are twisted. Knob of stainless steel, base of oak.
Photo: Mick Maxen

Chapter 4: Patterns in Damascus Steel

Kitchen knife "Black Kitchen Mistress IV" by Gunther Löbach. Blade in cover layer technique of twisted explosion pattern Damascus (O2 / 1.2767) with a cutting layer of file steel. The ferrule is stainless steel, and the handle is ebony.

Vegetable knife "Black Kitchen Mistress III" by Gunther Löbach. Blade in cover layer technique of twisted spirograph Damascus (O2 / 15N20) with a cutting layer of file steel. The ferrule is stainless steel, and the handle is ebony.

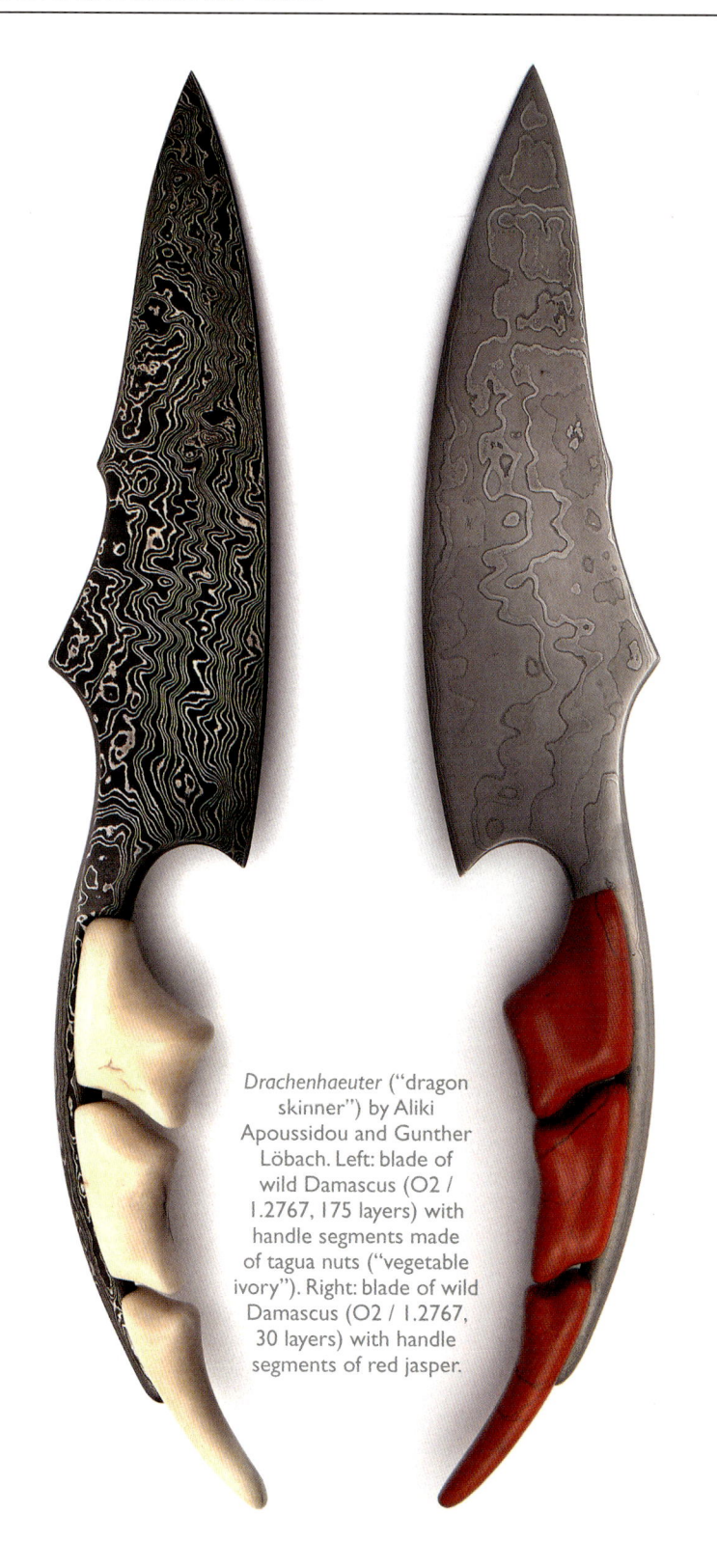

Chapter 4: Patterns in Damascus Steel

Drachenhaeuter ("dragon skinner") by Aliki Apoussidou and Gunther Löbach. Left: blade of wild Damascus (O2 / 1.2767, 175 layers) with handle segments made of tagua nuts ("vegetable ivory"). Right: blade of wild Damascus (O2 / 1.2767, 30 layers) with handle segments of red jasper.

Chapter 4: Patterns in Damascus Steel

This sickle for harvesting herbs was a custom order. Between the tip and the handle, the bar from which the sickle was forged remains part of the piece.
Photo: Martin Steinhorst

"Fan" knives by Gunther Löbach. Striped Damascus from O2 and 1.2767, nine layers.

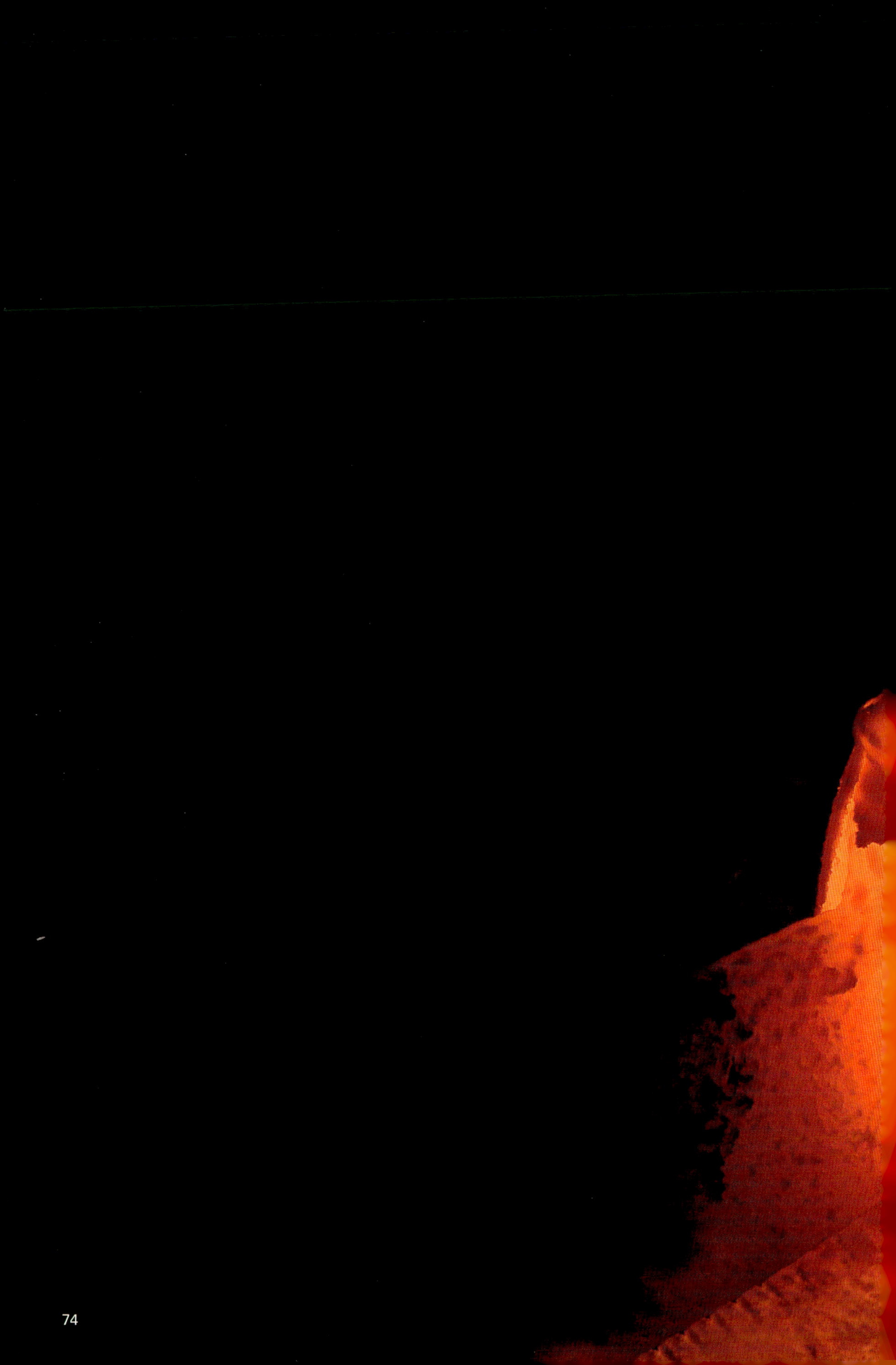

Part II: Practice

Chapter 5: Damascus in Practice

Damascus in Practice

5.1 Many Ways to the Destination

The production of pattern-welded steel is a very complex task. To carry it out successfully, you have to pay attention to a multitude of factors. In addition, there are many ways to reach the same goal. This becomes more obvious when reading the various resources that contain practical instruction. Each author has his/her own ways of approaching the goal, their own wisdom and tricks which may even contradict each other. Thus it is really up to everyone involved in Damascus steel and its production to find out which working method is best for himself/herself by conducting their own experimentation.

The following processes and tips are the result of my own work with Damascus steel. They were created over a span of several years and are quite successful. But I am far from describing them as the "only truth"—by means of new insights, tools, and materials, without doubt, they will continue to evolve.

I would like to encourage everybody to discover and try different paths by studying the relevant literature, and engaging in conversations with other Damascus smiths about their own experiences. By combining these experiences, everyone can find the "right" way for themselves. Besides that, I also want to motivate you all to share the gained knowledge with others in return.

The following practical tips are meant as an aid for beginners. They ought to help in choosing materials, techniques, and methods. The described selection is meant to minimize the risk of failure and achieve a successful result by means of work steps that are as simple as possible.

For the production of welded Damascus, many work steps are necessary during which as much as possible has to be done the "right" way in order to achieve a satisfying (i.e., flawless) result. Since it is very difficult for a beginner to keep an eye on all the many factors and to exclude all sources of error, failures (welding errors, cracks due to overheating the billet, etc.) are very likely to occur. With respect to the complexity of the process, this is not surprising. You shouldn't let yourself become discouraged by this. Even Damascus smiths with several decades of experience make mistakes every once in a while.

With respect to this great deal of effort, failures that render a workpiece useless in the end are especially annoying. For this reason, every work step should be followed with the greatest possible attention and care. The safest way to the goal is to systematically exclude or minimize all the possible sources of failure. Hereby impatience and haste are totally out of place. If, in the end, the workpiece turns out to be useless, many times the amount of, presumably saved, time has to be invested into producing a new piece. Surely the process can be quickened noticeably by routine and experience. But for beginners, I recommend not looking at the time, but instead work towards a successful result.

Chapter 5: Damascus in Practice

Forge welding with an air hammer.

Chapter 5: Damascus in Practice

5.2 Safety at Work

There can never be too much content on the important topic of work safety. The various work steps contain a series of hazards which require precautions. Metalworkers are surely familiar with many of these issues, but a few should be pointed out here.

5.2.1 Forge Welding

Here the biggest risk is from the molten flux which, together with unwanted oxides and impurities, can squirt out between the steel layers when they are welded together by hammer blows. This hot slag cools down much slower than forging scale or other glowing particles, and thus easily burns holes into clothes, glasses, skin, or other sensitive objects. Depending on the working method, glowing droplets can fly up to sixteen feet. Thus, it is important to shield individuals and sensitive objects from flying slag by using personal protective garments or shielding (e.g., erected hardboards).

Besides that, the noise pollution is high, especially when using a power hammer, and the constant observation of the welding billet in the bright fire in the long run damages the eyes due to ultraviolet radiation. Thus, the following protective measures should be taken during forge welding:

- Wear protective glasses (tinted, look for protection against ultraviolet radiation)
- Wear protective gloves
- Wear ear protection (especially when working with a power hammer)
- Point out the dangers of flying slag to others: if possible, protect them with "shielding walls."

5.2.2 Grinding / Polishing

To make the pattern of the Damascus steel visible, in most cases you can't get around grinding off some of the material. For this, take the usual precautions for doing abrasive work. This is especially important when working with nickel or steel containing nickel, since this element and

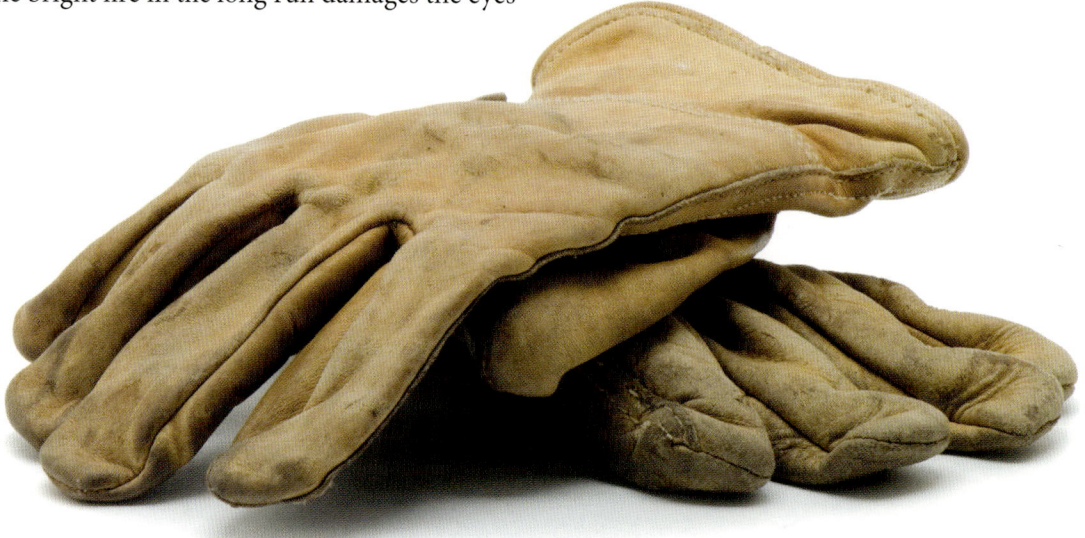

Leather gloves protect the hands from flying slag.

Chapter 5: Damascus in Practice

its compounds are allergenic, carcinogenic, and, above a certain concentration, also toxic. While grinding, you ought to show consideration for other people in your workshop. The following precautions should be taken for grinding and polishing:

- Wear protective glasses
- Wear a respirator or dust mask
- Wear ear protection

Untinted protection goggles.

5.2.3 Working with Acids

Of the three etching agents described later, sulfuric acid is much more corrosive and more dangerous than citric acid or ferric chloride. The latter causes ugly spots and is toxic as soon as it comes into contact with copper or copper alloys, but the danger of burns is rather low. For dilution of acids, always remember to pour acid into water, because whenever you add water to concentrated acid, it produces a violent, gaseous reaction, during which the dangerous fluid may spray. Thus always use the reverse method: pour acid into water in a thin stream!

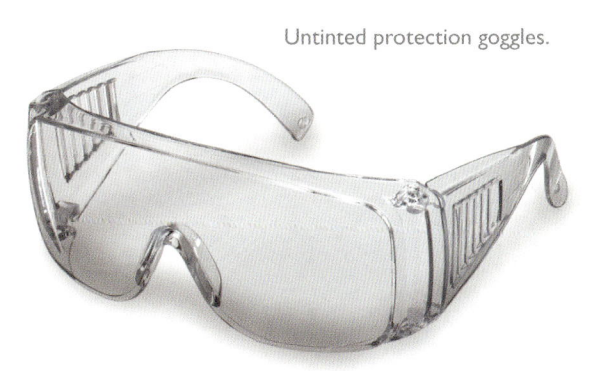

In addition, good ventilation is necessary. The best solution is to work directly beneath an extraction fan or outdoors. To neutralize spilled acid, a substance such as baking soda should be readily available in case of an emergency. When working with acids, the following preventive measures should be taken:

- Wear protective glasses (even better: a face shield)
- Wear protective gloves (resistant to acids)
- Wear an apron
- Assure good ventilation
- Have the necessary substances for neutralizing acids on hand

Ear protection.

Chapter 6: Materials

Materials

In general, welded Damascus consists of two or more different steel types (see Chapter 1.1), which differ with respect to their carbon content and/or other alloy elements. A special case is provided by pure nickel, which can also be forge welded to materials with an iron base.

To describe the extensive metallurgical background of the individual influential factors in detail is beyond the scope of this book. Here, the emphasis is put on practical processes. For these reasons, I will only mention the effects which are directly relevant to the production of welded Damascus (because they influence the weldability and the color). To readers with a great interest in this topic I recommend the book *Knife Blades and Steel* ("*Messerklingen und Stahl*"), by Roman Landes (see bibliography).

6.1 Carbon Content

An extremely important factor is the carbon content of the raw materials. The carbon content is of central importance because it determines how the steel behaves during welding as well its reactivity with respect to acids.

6.1.1 Welding Qualities

The carbon content determines the minimum welding temperature [T_{min}] of the raw material: i.e., the temperature, once reached, at which the material can be fused by forge welding. There exists an inversely proportional dependency: the higher the carbon content, the lower the T_{min}.

Furthermore, the carbon content also determines the temperature the material can endure before

Various flat sections of basic material for layered Damascus.

Chapter 6: Materials

the carbon burns up and causes cracks and partial decarburization [T_{max}]. Here the dependency is also inversely proportional: the higher the carbon content, the lower the T_{max}.

These two values frame the temperature window within which a given material can be forge welded. If materials with a different carbon content are to be combined, the whole billet has to be inside the overlapping area of both (or all) temperature windows to become successfully welded. This means, for combinations with very different carbon contents, the overlapping area is very small, which in turn makes a successful weld more difficult.

6.1.2 Carbon Diffusion

Within the material structure, carbon strives to distribute itself as evenly as possible. Thus it "wanders" from places with high concentration to areas with lower concentration. The higher the temperature of the material, the quicker this carbon diffusion takes place.

To achieve multi-layered Damascus, the material almost always has to be heated repeatedly to welding temperature. In addition, the layers become thinner—this means, the distance carbon has to move becomes shorter. Since during forging Damascus steel is exposed to very high temperatures over a certain period of time, it can be assumed for a relatively thin-layered superstructure that the carbon content becomes totally homogenized. In the past, this effect was used in the production of refined steel (see chapter 1.4.1).

6.1.3 Colors / Shading

The carbon content also influences the etching behavior of a material. In case the structure is rather coarse and the carbon content not homogenized, its components react to acid in a different way. Materials with high carbon content are corroded to a higher extent than those with a lower carbon content. For short etching times, this becomes obvious in the color: for longer times, a noticeable relief is created. The latter effect can be used to brighten the elevated portions by means of final sanding or polishing and thus to enhance the contrast and, if the occasion arises, to integrate shadows, which emphasize the plasticity (see 3.3.2).

The color contrast created by the different carbon contents is rather subtle—it is made from various shades of gray. To achieve strong contrasts, the materials must contain additional alloying elements.

6.2 Other Alloying Elements

The alloying elements most interesting, with respect to aesthetics, are manganese (Mn) and nickel (Ni). The many other additions mostly affect the mechanical properties of the material. Their influence on weldability and colorization by means of etching, in contrast, is quite low. An exception is chromium (Cr), which, above a certain concentration, turns traditional forge welding into an impossible task (more on this soon).

6.2.1 Manganese

Manganese is responsible for the dark color of the material during etching and thus is suitable for creating high contrasts with a steel type rich in carbon. Furthermore, the addition of manganese enhances the weldability and the ability to thoroughly harden the material.

6.2.2 Nickel

Nickel is the counterpart to manganese. This material reacts with the acid in a weaker way and thus keeps its lighter color. Besides that, its metallic luster is kept longer during etching. Pure nickel is hardly affected by acids and often not corroded at all.

Nickel doesn't influence weldability. Nickel-alloy steels in general are relatively creep-resistant at elevated temperatures and are tougher during forging than the other materials mentioned. Because of this, they are less deformed than those

Chapter 6: Materials

previously discussed, a fact that has to be taken into account with respect to the thickness of layers. If all the layers ought to have the same thickness in the end, the source material containing nickel has to be a bit thinner than the other materials.

Nickel poses risks to your health, which means that the necessary safety precautions must be taken prior to its processing (see 5.2).

6.2.3 Chromium

During its heating, chromium reacts with the oxygen in the surrounding air to form chromium oxide, which prevents a successful fusion of the source materials. Materials with a significant chromium content (starting around two percent) thus can only be forge welded under specific conditions (inert gas atmosphere, vacuum).

6.3 Commonly Used Materials

An overview of the most important qualities of the frequently used materials is given in the table at the end of the book (see page 171). The introduced materials ought to help with the selection of materials from the vast amount of available steel alloys.

6.3.1 Tool Steel O2

This is a "classic" steel for welded Damascus because of its pronounced black appearance, its good weldability, and a carbon content useful for most applications. O2 is a "dark" steel type commonly used in cold work steel—it is available in many different shapes and sizes at a relatively modest price.

6.3.2 1070 and 1095

The steels of the 10xx series are relatively pure carbon steels with a slight addition of manganese. They can be welded easily. The two mentioned types are easy to get and are well suited for knifemaking with respect to their carbon content. Their colors are, due to their smaller manganese content, a bit less dark than that of O2 but nevertheless these steels are used as the dark component of Damascus by many smiths.

6.3.3 File Steel W2

Because of its extremely high carbon content, this material is hard to weld, but it is outstanding for high-performance cutting edges. For this reason it is used solely, or in combination with similarly performing steels, as the central layer of knives.

6.3.4 Ball Bearing Steel 52100

This material also has a very fine-grained structure and thus is well suited for high-end cutting edges. In combination with file steel, this steel can create a high-performance Damascus. For an in-depth view of the advantages of these materials for certain purposes, I once again recommend the book *Knife Blades and Steel* ("*Messerklingen und Stahl*") by Roman Landes.

6.3.5 Spring Steel AISI 9255

This material isn't well suited for welded Damascus. Its weldability is below average.

6.3.6 Mild Steel

Because of its very low carbon content, the welding temperature area of this steel is very high, which leads to problems when combining it with carbon-containing steels. The material can't be hardened and also has a rather indifferent color after etching. Its advantages are its good availability, low price, and the fact that this steel is very good-natured with respect to possible overheating. Nevertheless, it can't be recommended for training because you have to get used to a totally different temperature range when changing to materials with higher carbon content.

Chapter 6: Materials

6.3.7 15N20

15N20 is a nickel-alloy steel with carbon content similar to that of its "contrasting partner," O2, which simplifies welding these materials together. Because of the nickel content a pronounced color contrast is, however, still produced.

6.3.8 L6

This nickel-containing steel keeps a very light color during etching and thus can be used for creating strong contrasts. Its reduced chromium content makes forge welding a bit more difficult.

6.3.9 Pure Nickel

If the end result is an especially strong contrast and not all the components have to be hardened (e.g., for jewelry or decorative Damascus which is put onto the cutting layer of a blade using the cover layer technique), then nickel is perfectly suited. It is (almost) not corroded by acid and even keeps its light, metallic luster with longer etching times.

Material Combinations

The following material combinations for different purposes have proven themselves in practice. They are arranged according to increasing grades of difficulty.

O2 + 15N20	O2 + L6	O2 + pure nickel	W2 + 52100
+ Good contrast of black and silver	+ Strong contrast of black and silver	+ Extreme contrast of black and silver	+ Suited for high-performance blades
+ Good weldability	– Modest weldability	– Not suited for blades (decorative Damascus)	– Difficult processing
			– Weak contrast

Damascus of O2 and 15N20.

Chapter 7: Heat Sources

Heat Sources

To heat the Damascus billet up to welding temperature—and also for heat treatment later on (soft annealing, hardening, tempering, etc.)—a heat source is needed. In the following I'll describe the three most common types and also their advantages and disadvantages.

7.1 Coal Forge

This traditional heat source was the only one available for millennia—it is the basic equipment of most forges. With a modicum of expertise you can build it yourself from scrap material at low cost. Tending a clean and evenly burning fire requires some training. During heating, coal has to be constantly charged, rearranged and, if need arises, moistened with water. With enough experience, the heat of the coal fire can be controlled selectively as well as over large areas.

To achieve the heat necessary for forging within a short amount of time, the use of sidewalls or even of a tunnel next to or over the fire place is recommended. This shielding reduces the loss of heat and allows the use of a smaller fire (and thus reduces the consumption of fuel). It can be built from fireclay bricks, concrete, or in the simplest case, from a piece of sheet metal bent to form an arch. Its dimensions should be large enough to allow tending the fire without going into contortions.

During forge welding, the fire should be kept very "clean," which means the fresh coal should not come into direct contact with the workpiece without shedding its sulfur content at the margins of the fire first. Furthermore, after each weld, the fire should be freed of slag and flux residues. After that, if necessary, fresh coal can be added to let the fire burn cleanly again.

Even more than during normal forging, the fire should be kept under control with water during forge welding. By regularly moistening the border areas, the embers are kept within the necessary zone. This way the consumption of fuel is drastically reduced and a huge flare up in the fire is prevented. Such a conflagration obstructs the view of the workpiece and its heat color and also makes work extremely unpleasant.

For fuel, forge coal, charcoal, or coke can be used. Charcoal burns more cleanly than the other fuels, but the consumption is relatively high. Some smiths use a mixture made from about a third of charcoal and two thirds forge coal.

The precise heat treatment of workpieces in the forging fire needs a lot of care, various auxiliary devices, and, most of all, a lot of experience. The effort and risk of failure climb exponentially with the size of the workpiece.

Chapter 7: Heat Sources

Coal Forge

Plus
- Low purchase cost
- Precise direction of heat
- Preheats quickly

Minus
- Forging area has a limited size
- Tending the fire requires great effort
- Difficult heat treatment
- Smoke and stench (to the delight of the neighbors!)
- Residues

The coal forge is the traditional heat source of a smith.

Chapter 7: Heat Sources

7.2 Gas Forge

A gas forge usually consists of a metal cylinder that is insulated on the inside with chamotte, ceramic wool, and/or kiln mortar and is fuelled by one or more (propane) gas burners fitted to the cylinder. To achieve higher temperatures, the gas flame can be heated up with air being blown in.

You can build a gas forge without significant effort, too. But since this forge is fueled by a flammable gas under high pressure, compared to building a coal forge, a gas forge requires a lot more caution and expertise. The Internet has a multitude of detailed instructions on gas forges and the required precautions.

By means of separately regulating the supply of gas and air, the atmosphere within the combustion chamber can be adjusted. By creating a weakly reducing atmosphere (rich mixture), the oxidation of workpieces is kept to a minimum. But the forge needs a certain preheating time until the insulation has reached a constant temperature. Fine tuning the atmosphere should only be done after the working temperature has been achieved. With the help of a flame in front of the combustion chamber, it can be determined what kind of mixture exists inside the forge:

Blue flame = lean mixture (too much oxygen)
"No" flame = balanced mixture
"Blazing" yellow flames = rich mixture (not enough oxygen)

With the gas forge, tending to the fire as you have to do with the coal forge isn't necessary. After pre-heating, you can start working without any further effort after the intensity of the flame (i.e., the temperature) and the atmosphere are adjusted. Heating takes place more or less evenly in the whole combustion space. Selective heating, as with the coal forge, can't be achieved with a gas forge. This, in turn, has advantages: a gas forge is better for heat treatment of the finished workpieces. In addition, the time necessary for drawing out the workpiece is reduced because the billet is heated up over its whole length, and not section by section.

When burning great amounts of propane, correspondingly large amounts of CO_2 and water are created. Thus the ventilation in the work environment must be good (it's best to work outdoors), and proximity to objects sensitive to rusting (machines, tools, etc.) ought to be avoided.

Gas Forge

Plus
- Relatively low purchase cost
- Only minor oxidation of workpieces
- Low operating cost
- Fire doesn't require tending
- Suitable for heat treatment (with restrictions)

Minus
- Long preheating time
- No selective heat
- Potentially dangerous

Chapter 7: Heat Sources

A DIY gas forge. *Photo: Achim Wirtz*

Chapter 7: Heat Sources

7.3 Electric Oven

An electric oven with sufficiently precise temperature control allows targeted heating of workpieces without the danger of overheating. For this reason, several billets can be heated and worked with simultaneously, which drastically reduces the overall necessary work time. As with the gas forge, the complete heating of the billet is important because of the time needed for drawing out the workpiece.

The drawbacks of the electric oven are the very long preheating times and the slower heating of the workpieces, which results in the creation of more oxides. With the electric oven, too, selective heat cannot be achieved. Besides that, care has to be taken that the flux doesn't come into contact with the heat coils of the oven, because these would be corroded by the aggressive chemicals.

In addition, the purchase costs for a sufficiently large electric oven are quite high. And finally, not all oven models are rated to the needed temperatures of up to 2,190°F (1,200°C).

Electric Oven

Plus
- Even and precise heating of workpieces
- No danger of overheating
- Several billets can be heated at the same time
- No direct environmental pollution or residues
- Well suited for heat treatment

Minus
- High purchase cost
- Relatively high operating costs
- Increased creation of oxides
- No selective heat

Chapter 7: Heat Sources

An electric oven has several pros and cons compared to the forges featuring open fire.

Chapter 8: Power Sources

Power Sources

8.1 Handheld Hammer

The classic method of forging with a handheld hammer is strenuous and time-consuming, but at the same time it is very precise and allows good control. Through the light blows of a hammer (compared to a power hammer), the Damascus billet becomes only slightly thinner during welding, which is an advantage if you need a thicker cross-section for your object from the outset.

Since speed is essential, because of how quickly the steel cools down, consider a rather light hammer ~2.25–4.5 lbs (1.0–2.0 kg) for making a series of rapid, well-aimed blows. A slightly domed striking face helps to distribute the pressure favorably (slag and flux are pushed from the center to the sides).

The blows should be set overlapping and cover the whole surface of the billet. Start at one end (any end) and work along the length of the billet. Hereby the billet may have to be heated to forging temperature again every now and then.

If a power hammer is available, leave the main work for this tool. Delicate and selective welds as well as the correction of flaws and delaminations (open gaps between the layers), in contrast, can be done very well and in a controllable way with the handheld hammer.

8.2 Power Hammer

Forge welding with a spring or air hammer needs a bit of training, but saves a lot of time and energy. While the machine doesn't provide any significant advantage with respect to the duration of welding per se, this becomes noticeable when drawing out of the billet. The process of drawing out is an ever-recurring work step for increasing the number of layers.

The shape of the forging dies should be spherical (dome-shaped) in one direction. You have to take care that the dies are fastened in a way that the fit exactly. A dent in the center caused by wear can lead to unwelded "blisters" inside the billet, since the borders connect first and the escape of the flux is thus blocked.

Forging with a handheld hammer is versatile and allows for good control, but it is strenuous.

Chapter 8: Power Sources

In conclusion,: a power hammer doesn't necessarily lead to better welds, but it means a drastic reduction of work time.

8.3 Hydraulic Press

A hydraulic press has various advantages and disadvantages compared to the two previously mentioned tools. Since it transfers its power relatively slowly onto the workpiece, the forging dies are in contact with the surface of the billet for a relatively long time, which in turn causes a somewhat quick loss of heat (especially from the cover layers). This problem is more pronounced for thinner layers than for thick ones. For a successful weld, the forging dies should thus be preheated. This can be done by means of a steel block that is heated and clamped into the press for a couple of minutes prior to the actual welding. Other possibilities to reduce the loss of heat are forging dies or intermediate layers of a material with lower thermal conduction (titanium, for example).

For the hydraulic press, too, at least one of the forging dies should be slightly domed to prevent the creation of blisters by welding the border areas first (see chapter 11.7 for this as well).

A hydraulic press is extremely well suited for the work step of "packing" prior to the actual welding (see 11.3). If all the layers are pressed flat on top of each other, a good deal of the mixture of flux and oxides is squeezed out at this point.

A power hammer saves a lot of time and force, but doesn't necessarily lead to better weldings.

Chapter 8: Power Sources

8.4 Other Possibilities

Besides these three sources of power, some other lesser known methods can be used as well. One of them is the eccentric press. In principle, this is similar to a power hammer but the force is transferred onto the workpiece not with springs, but by means of a large flywheel mass and a gear that manages very high forces. Depending on the construction of such a press, the distance between the forging dies has to be set to the thickness of the material (approximately), which should be done prior to heating up the workpiece to forging temperature so as not to lose any time during those decisive moments.

With a forging roll, forge welding can also be done. As with the eccentric press, the suitability also strongly depends on the construction and the drive of the roll. This machine has to be adjusted even more precisely than the eccentric press to the thickness of the workpiece.

A hydraulic press is easy to control and not very noisy.

Chapter 9: Auxiliary Materials

Auxiliary Materials

9.1 Flux

For successful forge welding, a flux is needed for two reasons: to remove oxide layers from the workpiece, and to form a glassy protective cover that protects the billet from contact with oxygen and thus from further creation of oxides. The flux melts on the surface of the metal and, due to capillary action, moves between the layers of the unwelded billet where it starts to detach the oxides. During "packing" (see 11.3) and later welding, the flux is squeezed out from in between the layers together with the detached oxides.

Which kind of flux ought to be used is a controversial question. Diverse sources advocate very different opinions with respect to this problem. But in general it can be said that the choice depends on the welding temperature and thus on the carbon content of the used materials.

9.1.1 Glass Sand (Silicon Dioxide SiO_2)

The traditional flux is glass sand, which has very high working temperatures and thus should only be used for welding mild steel and other materials with low carbon content.

9.1.2 Borax (Disodium Tetraborate $Na_2[B_4O_5(OH)_4]$)

For tool steels with a higher percentage of carbon and other alloying elements, borax has proven itself well. Since borax tends to absorb water from the surrounding air, which is detrimental to the welding, it ought to be kept sealed from air. Borax is available from goldsmith suppliers and also in large quantities from agricultural suppliers.

Borax is available as powder or granules.
It should be kept dry and sealed from air.

Chapter 9: Auxiliary Materials

Ferric chloride must be mixed with water prior to its use. It should be kept sealed from air.

9.1.3 Mixtures and Additives

In various sources a mixture of ten parts borax and one part ammonium chloride (NH_4Cl) is recommended. For difficult welds which can't be fixed via arc welding for technical reasons or which contain many pores (e.g., saw chains), the flux can be mixed 1:1 with mild steel filings. This mixture acts like a weak "glue."

9.2 Etching Substances

9.2.1 Ferric Chloride ($FeCl_3$)

This substance is commonly used for etching circuit boards and artistic etchings. Compared to sulfuric acid, it is rather harmless and the etching process is slower and thus more controllable. Furthermore, it doesn't have to be warmed up and lasts quite long. Copper and its alloys shouldn't come into contact with the etching bath because a layer of copper will settle onto every iron-containing material etched in the same bath later on.

The substance is available as granules. A good mixture in practice is one part of $FeCl_3$ with three parts of water. Depending on the used materials and the desired depth of etching, the etching period can last between five and forty-five minutes. Ferric chloride can be obtained from vendors for electronics manufacturers or companies selling supplies for artists.

9.2.2 Sulfuric Acid (H_2SO_4)

Sulfuric acid with a concentration of about 30 to 40 percent and is suitable for etching Damascus. It can be purchased as battery acid for cars and warmed up in a water bath to 120°F (50°C). Compared to ferric chloride, etching is done much quicker: when using fresh, heated acid, a period of 30 to 120 seconds is usually sufficient. The acid loses its effectiveness quickly and then has to be renewed. Because of volatile by-products, etching with sulfuric acid should only be done with good ventilation (outdoors).

Chapter 9: Auxiliary Materials

Sulfuric acid can be bought at car supply shops. Used sulfuric acid has to be treated as hazardous waste; it should not be disposed of with other household waste.

9.2.3 Citric Acid ($C_6H_8O_7$)

This relatively weak, and rather harmless, acid is usually found in the household (for decalcification). You can obtain citric acid in drugstores, for example. Similar to sulfuric acid, it is warmed up to 120°F and can then be used for etching Damascus. But citric acid only creates a contrast in color; it is not possible to etch reliefs with this acid.

Battery acid can be used for etching Damascus without further thinning.

Citric acid is easy to obtain and relatively free of danger. But it is not suitable for etching reliefs.

Chapter 10: Preparing the Billet

Preparing the Billet

Prior to the start of forge welding, some preparations are necessary. These steps will make later work easier and are needed for creating a flawless composite of the materials.

10.1 Dimensions of the Billet

For ease of work, the maximum length of the billet should be about 4 inches (100 millimeters). At this length the whole billet can be welded (with a power hammer) during a single work step before the temperature sinks too low. Besides that, if you use a coal forge, it is difficult to heat longer billets evenly. This problem doesn't exist with gas forges or electric ovens, but the welding of longer billets should in any case be done in several, overlapping steps while heating up the billet to welding temperatures time and again. Very short billets (shorter than 2.3 inches [60 mm]) can be worked on without problems, but since a certain loss occurs over its length (see section 13.3), they should be drawn out in length.

To have enough material for larger objects, several billets can be produced and welded together during the last round of folding. Hereby the strenuous step-by-step procedure is limited to a single welding process.

The broader the billet becomes, the greater the danger that the borders will be welded first while unwelded blisters are created in the center. For

Pieces of sheet metal prepared for a laminate billet.

Chapter 10: Preparing the Billet

smaller billets, this problem hardly exists, but, of course, you have less material. In practice, a width of 1.125 to 1.5 inches (30 to 40 millimeters) has proven itself to be a good compromise. This measurement should also be kept for further welds after the initial one. Naturally, the billet becomes a bit broader when it is drawn out—this should be corrected before it is folded or cut for another weld.

The height of the billet ought to be the same as its width to facilitate even heating. If necessary, increase the height by adding more layers before making the billet broader or longer. With power hammers in particular, welding thicker billets is not a problem because of the hammer's power of impact. An ideal maximum billet height is 2.3 inches (60 millimeters).

Tip

- Length of the billet 2.3–4 inches (60–100 mm)
- Width of the billet 1.125–1.5 inches (30–40 mm)
- Height of the billet 1.125–4 inches (30–60 mm)

Recommended size of a Damascus billet.

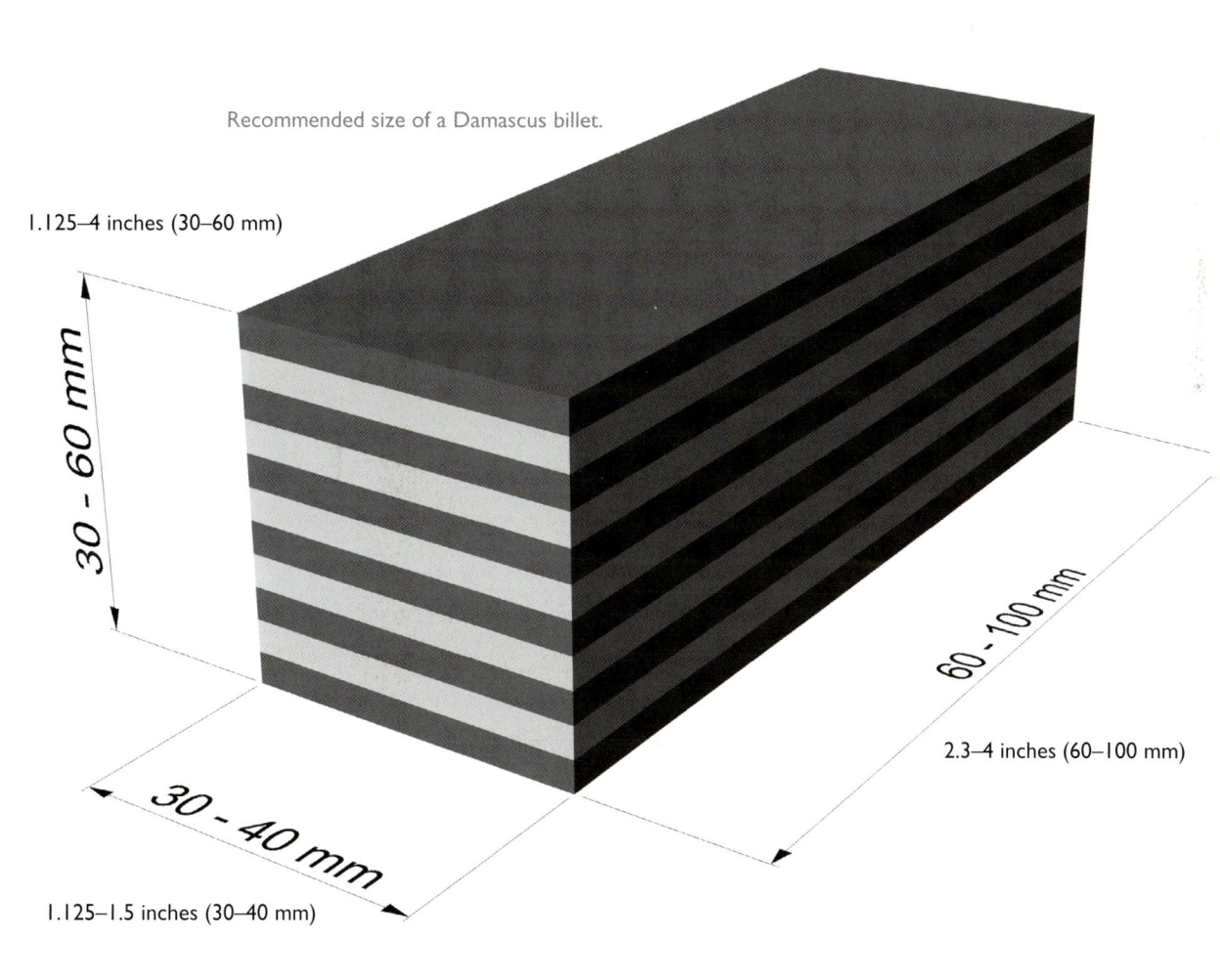

1.125–4 inches (30–60 mm)
30 – 60 mm
30 – 40 mm
1.125–1.5 inches (30–40 mm)
60 – 100 mm
2.3–4 inches (60–100 mm)

Chapter 10: Preparing the Billet

10.2 Number of Layers and Their Arrangement

To best avoid problems during heating, use a symmetrical structure, which means an odd number of layers with the cover layers made from the same material. If the number of layers is to be increased by multiplication (see chapter 13), then it makes sense to put the material with the lowest content of chromium on the outside—this lessens the danger of errors during the later welds. With the chromium-poor steel on the outside during later packing, an even number of pieces can be used for later welds.

Two layers of pure nickel cannot easily be welded together. Thus they should not be used as cover layers if the number of layers is to be increased later on by folding or stacking. Using these methods for increasing the number of layers, two layers of the same material are always welded together, thus creating an optically thicker layer, which may disrupt the pattern. The fewer layers the billet has in the beginning, the denser these zones lie next to each other. From a certain number of layers onwards (with correspondingly thin layers), the difference in layer thickness is no longer obvious.

To avoid this effect, a structure with an even number of layers and thus different cover layers must be used. Additionally, in this case the number of layers can only be increased by stacking, not folding. Hereby care should be taken that the pieces all have the same orientation during stacking—mark one of the longitudinal edges of the billet prior to dividing it (also see chapter 13).

The thickness of the individual layers is usually determined by the dimensions of the available semi-finished products. Here, there is no technical difference regardless of the used thickness as long as the layers are not too thin (less than 0.05 inches [1.5 mm]). The thinner the single layers are, the slower the billet ought to be heated to avoid warping by different expansion rates of the individual layers.

Not all the layers have to be of the same thickness. Just the opposite: for certain patterns it can be attractive, for example, to combine thin layers of nickel-steel with thick layers of manganese-steel. This results in fine, bright lines on a dark surface.

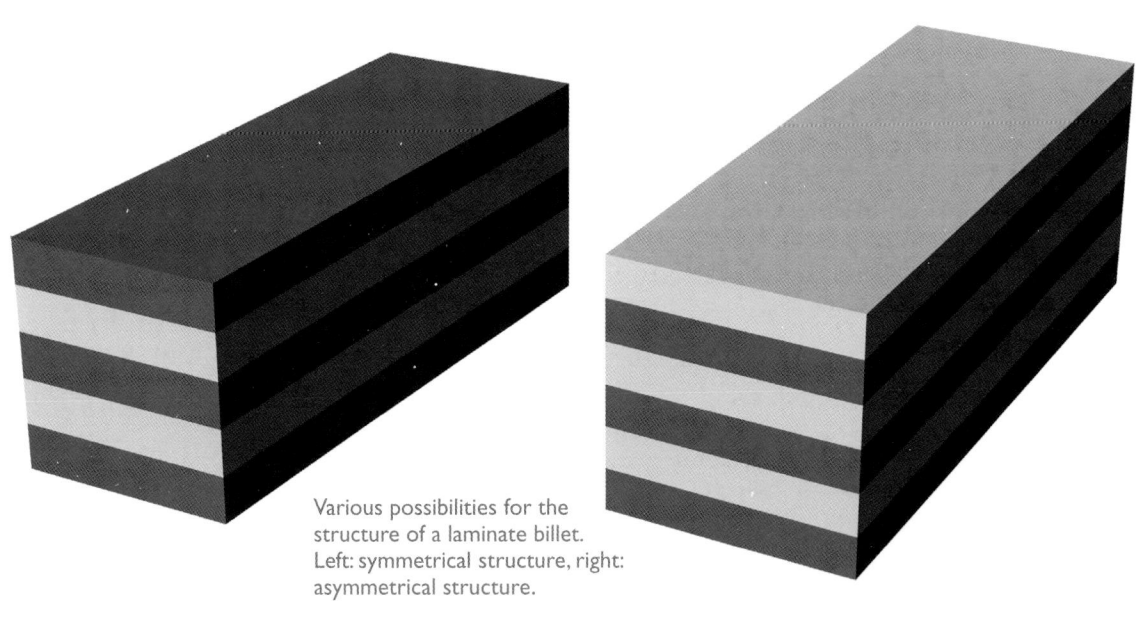

Various possibilities for the structure of a laminate billet. Left: symmetrical structure, right: asymmetrical structure.

Chapter 10: Preparing the Billet

Among these possibilities, the number of the initial layers is, of course, dependent on how many layers the billet ought to have in the end. Some assistance with answering this question is given in chapter 13.

> **Tip**
>
> - Use an uneven number of layers and a symmetrical structure.
>
> - Steel with low chromium content works best as cover layers.
>
> - The thickness of each layer should be more than 0.08 inches (2.0 mm).
>
> - The overall thickness of the billet should be 1.125 to 4 inches (30–60 mm).

10.3 Preparing the Surfaces

The surface of the areas which have to be welded should always be bright and metallic (this means free of forging scale and dirt) and, if possible, also flat and level. The latter is hard to achieve after the first welding without partially grinding the uppermost layers, which shows up as an error within the pattern later on.

In principle, the surface can be smoothed via grinding or sandblasting. Creating evenly ground surfaces is always preferable to sandblasting because they reduce the probability of welding errors.

When using flat sections or strips of sheet metal as raw material, first evenly grind the steel, then cut it to pieces—this way it is easier to hold the material. A sharp and relatively coarse belt ought to be used (grit P60–P80) for grinding. If cut pieces are to be ground, then (especially for thin material) use a wooden slab to make sure the piece doesn't get jammed in the belt. With magnets (e.g., from speakers) as "handles," the flat pieces can also be ground easily on a plane surface. The roughness of the surface caused by grooves from grinding is no problem. On the contrary, it allows oxides to be swept away by the flux. To aid this oxide removal process, the pieces should be ground laterally or diagonally.

Since the surface of the billet is rarely completely flat after the first welding, there is the danger that individual layers are partially abraded during grinding. This really can't be avoided for very thin layers. With wild Damascus the created "errors" are not necessarily detrimental to the overall image. But for patterns which are attractive because of their exactness, no further grinding should be done after the first weld. Instead, the surface can be freed from oxides by sandblasting. This ought to be done thoroughly. Steels containing nickel are especially susceptible to building up a very tough layer of oxides, which can be very difficult to remove with sandblasting.

Another method for removing forging scale is to put the steel into vinegar (acetic acid at 20–25%). Depending on the thickness of the forging scale, this process can take several hours and is best done over night.

> **Tip**
>
> - Prior to the first welding, grind the raw material (flat section) on the belt sander (grit P80) laterally or diagonally to a flat and shiny state.
>
> - Prior to all further weldings, forge the billet as smooth and flat as possible, then sandblast.
>
> - To save time, you can omit working on the outside (cover) layers.

Chapter 10: Preparing the Billet

Grinding flat material to a sheen is relatively easy prior to cutting. It ought to be ground diagonally.

Chapter 10: Preparing the Billet

When grinding small pieces, hold them with magnets.

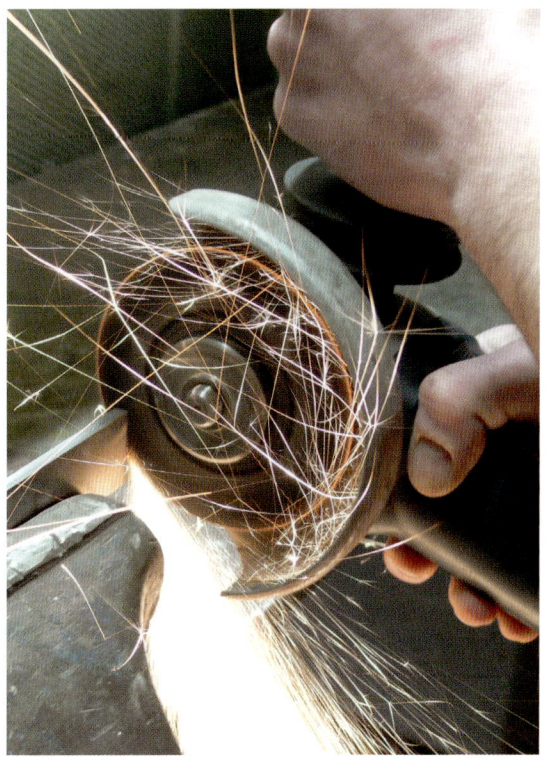

Cut the sections into equally long pieces with the angle grinder.

The surface can be cleaned of scale by sandblasting.

Chapter 10: Preparing the Billet

10.4 Fixing & Adding a Handle

The individual layers now have to be stacked into a billet and fixed. The use of binding wire, which was traditionally recommended by some, is unnecessarily awkward if you have access to arc welding equipment. Though tack-welding has a disadvantage in that part of the material melts and a certain amount then has to be cut off, the reduced workload more than compensates for this loss. Experience shows that the quality of the welds is usually worse at the ends of the billet. If the ends are cut off prior to renewed stacking, the danger of delamination lessens (there are no gaps enhancing the probability of weld shear).

It is recommended that you weld on a handle so that working with the billet is easier. A flat piece of steel that is about 1.125 wide and 0.196 inches tall (30 × 5 mm) welded diagonally onto one end of the billet works best. In contrast to a handle made from round or square stock and fixed in the center, this diagonally fixed handle has the advantage of following the diagonal axis—it only gets twisted when the billet is forged flat. A round or square shape of similar dimensions becomes thinner at its ends with each hammer blow and doesn't have the necessary stability at yellow-hot temperatures.

How long the handle is made depends on the surroundings (type of forge, etc.) and also on personal preferences. Lengths between 20 and 30 inches (50 and 80 cm) work well. If using an electric oven for heating, weld a short piece (2.5–3.25 inches [6–8 cm]) that can be handled with tongs.

The stack is compiled, oriented, and held together with a C-clamp.

Chapter 10: Preparing the Billet

Tip

- Stack the layers, align them properly, and fix the billet with a C-clamp.

- At the center of one end, draw a tack weld perpendicular to the orientation of the layers via MIG/MAG or arc welding.

- Weld a flat piece of steel (about 24 × 1.125 × 0.196 inches [600 × 30 × 5 mm]) diagonally to the opposite face end for a handle. If this doesn't fix all the layers in place, extend the weld until it reaches the corners of the end face.

- If the (cover) layers of the billet are thin (less than 0.118 inches [3.0 mm]), draw a weld across all the layers in each corner instead; attach the handle as described above.

Thin materials ought to be connected at all four corners with welds.

Chapter 10: Preparing the Billet

With thicker pieces, a single weld in the center is sufficient.

Very thick materials can be secured with individual tacking dots.

Chapter 10: Preparing the Billet

If the handle is made of flat material, it ought to be attached diagonally.

Chapter 11: Forge Welding

Forge Welding

If the billet is prepared as described, you can start with actual forge welding. Prior to that, make sure that everything necessary is close at hand because any interruption during the welding process is extremely disruptive. Prepare the following:

- Forge with clean fire, already heated to temperature
- Prepared billet with a handle
- Flux
- Hammer and (if available) power hammer with appropriate forging dies
- Steel brush, small fire shovel, and water dispenser
- All safety precautions

11.1 Pre-Heating the Billet

Before doing anything, the billet has to be pre-heated. This means heated to the usual forging temperature. This should be done slowly and evenly. The thinner the individual layers are, the more time you should reserve for the task in order to avoid warping due to differential heating of the layers.

Place the billet into the fire so that the layers are standing upright. Then regularly and quickly turn the billet 180°. When heat colors start to show up, apply the first amount of flux (see 11.2).

Under moderate air supply, further heat the billet until all layers show a light red color (~1650–1740°F [900–950°C]). Here you have to take into account that, despite the vertical orientation, the cover layers heat up significantly faster than the interior ones. Avoid overheating at all cost! Sprinkle the cover layers with water if necessary.

With a gas forge or electric oven, even heating is much easier, as long as the temperature is set correctly. However, it does take longer for the billet to be thoroughly heated.

Tip

- Put the billet into the coal forge with the layers oriented vertically.

- Adjust the air supply to medium.

- Heat the billet, while regularly turning it 180°, until all layers show a light red color.

Heat the billet slowly until all layers have reached forging temperature.

Chapter 11: Forge Welding

11.2 Applying the Flux

Apply the flux by either strewing by hand or, perhaps with better aim and a higher regard for safety, by means of a small shovel. Keep the flux in a (fireproof!) bowl next to the forge so it can be accessed quickly and easily. Apply the powder to the edges of the vertically oriented layers. At first, bubbles will form, then it melts to form a glassy smelt that moves in between the layers. Now flip the billet 180° and repeat the process on the other side. The billet should be completely covered by melted flux.

For a medium size billet (see 10.1) use about 0.125–0.185 cubic inches (2–3 cubic centimeters) of flux per surface—if in doubt, it's better to use a little more than not enough.

Tip

- Upon reaching the pre-heated temperature, apply the flux from both sides onto the longer edges of the billet.

- When the flux is molten and covers the billet completely, you can start "packing."

With a small fire shovel, apply the flux directly onto the billet.

Chapter 11: Forge Welding

11.3. Packing

To minimize the gaps between the layers prior to welding, and to achieve complete contact between surfaces, the billet has to be compressed ("packed") at forging temperature. This way, small irregularities on the surfaces and warping are straightened out by heating.

This is especially recommended if the individual layers were not ground flat, which usually is the case if the billet is folded or stacked to increase the number of layers. For really plane and tightly stacked layers, you can forego packing.

For packing, the billet is forged over with blows from a really heavy hammer (7 to 9 lbs [3 to 4 kg]). During this process, you have to make certain that the opposite billet end doesn't open while you are working on the other.

A hydraulic press is very effective for "packing" the billet, because its pressure on the entire surface area prevents the layers from opening.

Chapter 11: Forge Welding

To avoid creating blisters in the center of the billet during welding, you can also forge the longitudinal edges a bit thinner (here, 0.039 to 0.078 inches [one to two millimeters] is sufficient!). By doing this, the force of the subsequent welding blows affects the center first and pushes flux and oxides towards the edges.

Another especially effective method is the use of a hydraulic press. Its high pressure squeezes the layers together. And, due to the distribution of its load over the entire area, a billet "gaping" at one end is avoided.

Tip

- After the flux has melted at forging temperature, squeeze the billet with a hydraulic press until a "belly" starts to form in the center.

- Bevel the shape of the billet down toward the longer edges slightly on both sides by forging over about 1/4 of the width of the billet. Forge this area down by about 0.039 inch. You don't have to flip the billet over to repeat this procedure on the opposite side.

To be sure that the force of the welding blows first acts upon the center, the edges of the billet can be flattened.

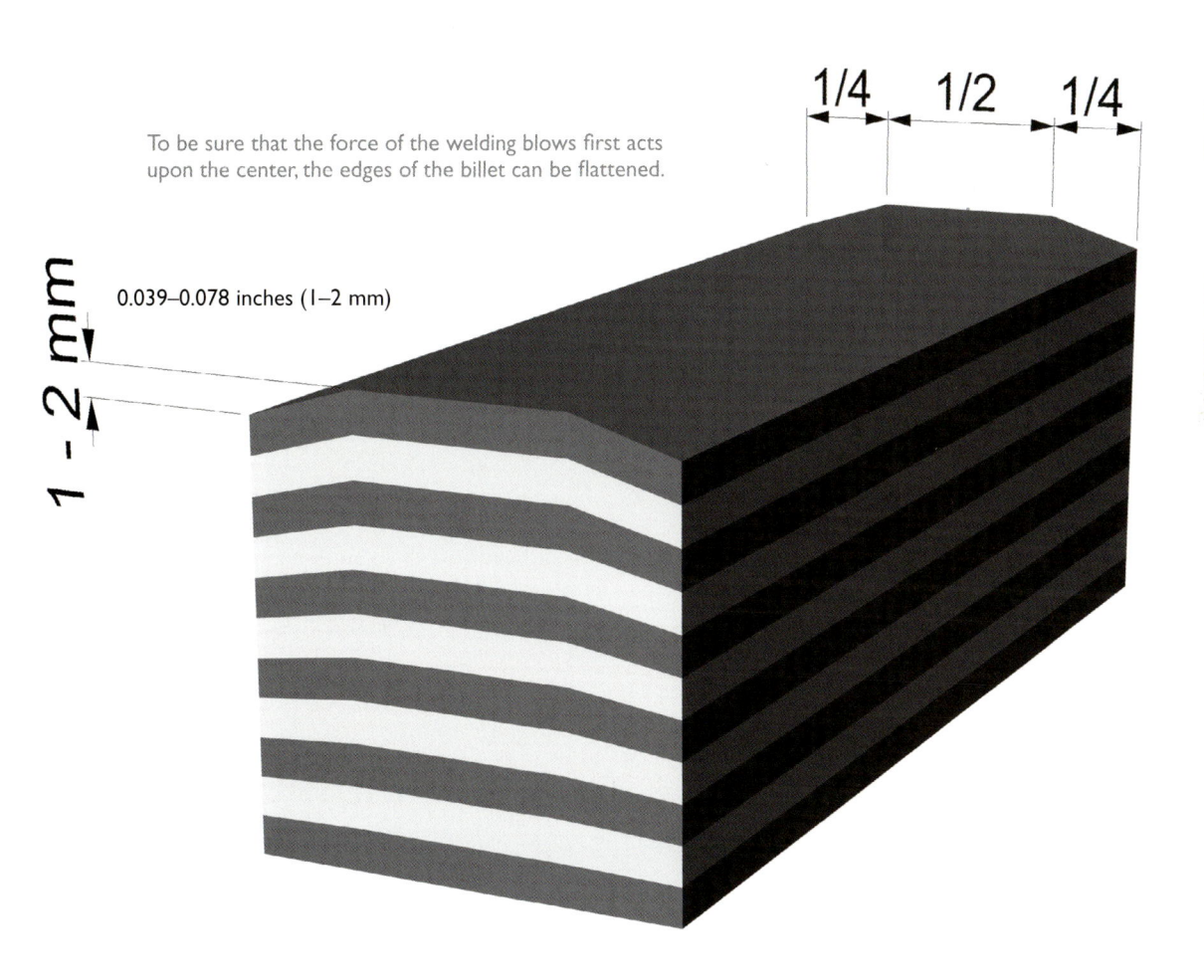

0.039–0.078 inches (1–2 mm)

1 - 2 mm

1/4   1/2   1/4

Chapter 11: Forge Welding

11.4 Heating to Welding Temperature

The "packed" billet can now be heated to welding temperature. The optimum temperature, depending on the carbon content of the material being used, lies between 1,920°F (1,050°C) (file steel; 1.45%C) and 2,190°F (1,200°C) (mild steel; less than 0.2%C). The greater the spread between the carbon content of the different materials to be welded together, the smaller the common temperature window.

If the material overheats, the carbon starts to burn, which can be recognized by the spraying and finely branched sparks, like a sparkler. This has to be avoided at all cost, since the decarburization accompanying this diminishes the performance of the steel and the material can also crack when overheated.

A billet which is only slightly overheated (displays a light yellow to whitish yellow heat color and solitary sparks) may be saved by letting it cool down for a couple of seconds—wait until the sparks are no longer emitted before starting to work on it. This way you may be able to avoid the creation of cracks.

A real "sparkler" with already molten areas usually is lost. In this case, the billet should be allowed to cool down, then carefully checked for cracks (grind it flat prior to that!) and all faulty areas must be removed by grinding or cutting to save at least part of the material.

For most steel types (carbon content between 0.4 and 1.0%) a welding temperature of about 2,015°F (1,100°C; dark yellow color) makes sense. Good evidence for this temperature is the reflective surface of the flux.

It is important to reach this temperature in the center of the billet as well. This is easy to achieve with gas forges and electric ovens. The feed of gas or temperature control is cautiously increased until welding temperature is reached. To ensure that this temperature also finds its way to the core, the billet subsequently ought to be heated for some more time.

If you use a coal forge, the billet has to be constantly turned—pack it after each 90° turn, instead of 180°. For this, it is helpful to follow a certain rhythm (e.g., count every three seconds.) Just before achieving the welding temperature, the frequency should be quickened to about once every second. When the surface of the billet reaches the welding temperature, this area can be cooled a bit by trickling or spraying some water on it (while the billet is still constantly being turned around). Thus the heat can penetrate to the core while the outer surfaces are brought back to welding temperature.

Tip

- With a medium air supply, heat up the billet with the layers oriented vertically, occasionally turning through 180° until all the layers show an orange heat color (1,740°–1,830°F [950–1,000°C]).

- Add flux once more and increase the air supply. Then turn the billet 90° every three seconds. When the heat color comes close to dark yellow, turn the billet at a quicker pace, 90° every second.

- When the surface of the billet reaches the welding temperature (about 2,015°F [1,100°C]), recognized by the dark yellow color and a slight reflection of the flux surface, sprinkle water on it while constantly turning the billet.

- Continue heating until the outer surfaces have reached welding temperature again.

Chapter 11: Forge Welding

The billet is heated to forging temperature while adding flux again.

Chapter 11: Forge Welding

11.5 Welding

During forge welding the materials are pressed together by mechanical pressure at the correct temperature. By this addition of energy, the border surfaces are briefly changed into a doughy condition and are fused.

As soon as the welding temperature is reached, the following work steps have to be done in rapid succession without wasting time: the temperature will quickly drop below the critical value and fusing the layers then is no longer possible. If this happens, the welding process has to be interrupted immediately and the billet has to be heated up again. In order to perform the motion sequence quickly and effectively during the decisive moments, I recommend first testing the procedure with a "dry run," i.e., with a cold billet.

To achieve a flawless and stable weld, the power of impact is not decisive. It is more important that the entire area is covered completely by (overlapping) hammer blows. Equally important is that the layers to be connected don't cool down below welding temperature during this process.

The mechanical work during forge welding can be done by hand or by means of machines as described in chapter 8. Independent of the procedures, to protect your tools, as much slag as possible ought to be removed from the outside of the billet before starting with the work.

This can be achieved by taking the billet out of the fire and banging it against the anvil horn. Hereby the layers ought to be oriented vertically to minimize deformation of the billet. The slag

Welding the billet with the power hammer. Depending on the working technique, slag and flux can fly off more…

Chapter 11: Forge Welding

can also be stripped off on a sharp edge (e.g., of the forge).

It is recommended to add a second "welding step" after the billet has been processed once completely. This way the created welds are stabilized and probable flaws can be corrected. For this, flux is applied once more (a good deal less is necessary this time because no gaps should be left for the flux to get into), and the billet is then again heated up to welding temperature and the forging is repeated.

Tip

- Weld the billet from one end to the other with quick, overlapping blows. During this process, drive the flux and slag away from you and out of the billet.

- If the temperature cools down too quickly, interrupt the welding process and heat the billet up to welding temperature again. Continue welding until the entire billet has been covered by hammer blows.

- To be on the safe side, add a second run.

…or less suddenly and dangerously.

Chapter 11: Forge Welding

11.6 Checking the Weld

To discover possible errors as quickly as possible, and to correct them as well, you must now check whether the layers are welded completely over their entire surfaces. Some welding errors can be spotted at first glance because the parts that are not welded or only partially welded cool down quicker than the rest of the billet (the heat streaming off the center is passed on much slower in areas with flawed welds than in those successfully fused together). The areas which are not connected firmly can be distinguished by their significantly darker heat color. But usually only errors which are relatively close to the outside of the billet (the cover layers) can be detected this way.

To check the central layers, the same condition (different rates of heat conduction for fused and unconnected layers) is analyzed, but in reverse: let the billet cool down until heat colors can't be distinguished anymore, then heat it up in the fire without turning the billet. Turn the layers horizontally. In this position the heat enters the billet mainly from the bottom.

After a certain amount of time, a consistent color gradient should be visible across the entire "height." If somewhere along the lateral surfaces significant steps in color appear, you can be quite sure that the layers at this spot are not fused correctly. This method, however, only works up to a point with gas forges and electric ovens because of the even heating from several sides.

Furthermore, flawed welds can also be recognized by grinding the face and/or lateral surfaces of the cold billet (grind perpendicular to the orientation of layers). After that, faulty parts are visible as barely recognizable, dark hair lines.

However, none of these methods can detect flaws that are close to the center of the billet and not in contact with the faces or lateral surfaces ("blisters").

Tip

- Heat the billet in the coal fire from one side and with the layers oriented horizontally.

- Check the color gradient on all sides.

By heating from one side, welding errors can be seen and localized. Here, the unwelded layers in the center as well as a small flaw in the area below are quite visible.

Chapter 11: Forge Welding

11.7 Welding Flaws

The two main problems that lead to the creation of welding flaws are:

- Low temperatures, too low for welding, which mainly happens in the center of the billet where the heat arrives "last."

- The inclusion of slag; this occurs when the layers connect at the borders first thus preventing flux and oxides from escaping (creation of blisters).

I'll next describe some methods for preventing and removing these flaws. Experience shows that the latter is only successful for some of the cases. Depending on the tools and auxiliaries being used, and on one's own method of working, an accumulation of specific flaws may occur. In this case, you should try to identify the causes and eliminate them in subsequent work.

11.7.1 Prevention of Flaws

If entirely or partially unwelded layers are detected, low temperatures are usually the cause. Mostly this affects welding gaps, which are close to the center of the billet, because the heat is applied from the outside and the core reaches the

Wear and tear causes dents on the dies, which should be removed by grinding every now and then.

Chapter 11: Forge Welding

desired temperature last. In such a case you ought to try to bring the billet to welding temperature more slowly and keep it there for a bit longer before you start welding. To avoid overheating during this phase, cool the outside of the billet by moistening with water. For gas forges and electric ovens, choose a correspondingly longer holding time.

If welding flaws over parts or entire layers can be seen around the outer layers as well, the most probable cause is a welding temperature which is genuinely too low. Before the layers are welded, more heat is radiated into the surroundings than can flow in from the core, especially during contact with anvil and dies, which have a much higher thermal conductivity than air. If the temperature of the billet is homogeneous but only slightly above that of the minimum welding temperature, the marginal areas rapidly cool down below the critical value, which means that fusion can't be achieved.

If during cooling a billet shows dark spots without connection to the border, which are visible on the cover layers, usually slag is enclosed. This means the borders of the layers connected first and the exit of flux was prevented. One reason for this can be concave wear of the used forging dies. This causes the force to be applied first and mainly onto the borders of the billet. The problem can be prevented by grinding the forging dies flat or by forging over the longitudinal edges after "packing."

Another possible cause may be concave contact areas of the individual layers. This cause can be eliminated from material that is ground flat, but sometimes shows up when stacking to increase the number of layers with sandblasted pieces. To avoid this problem, you ought to take care that when forging out the billet (see chapter 13.2) the later contact areas are forged flat during the final round. If the layers are worked on vertically (for example, to lessen the width of the billet), the workpiece is likely to mushroom, which has to be corrected during this final work step.

11.7.2 Correcting Flaws

Some faults can be corrected with the following methods. In other cases, too many oxides have formed on the critical surfaces, which render the rescue of the workpiece impossible. Nevertheless, in most cases it is at least worth one or two tries to fix the workpiece.

Completely or partly unconnected layers in some cases can be rescued by reheating the billet to welding temperature and rewelding. For this, flux again has to be applied generously at the open spots. Besides a sufficient holding period, you ought to try to achieve as high a temperature as possible without overheating.

During the rewelding of partially unconnected layers, you should always work from the "healthy" part towards the borders to push flux and oxides ahead of you towards the edge.

Encapsulated blisters have to be opened to squeeze out their contents. This is easiest done by means of a hot chisel. If the blister is close to a border of the billet, you can try to separate the layers at this place so that the inclusions can be pressed out of the billet horizontally. By using one-sided heating (as described in 11.6), pinpointing the layers between which the inclusion is located can be easily determined. During rewelding, flux should be applied generously and it should be worked into the direction of the open spot.

Blisters located centrally and close to the cover layers can be opened more easily by splitting the layers above at one end of the blister. This way the inclusions have the chance to leave vertically. Again, significant amounts of flux should be

Chapter 11: Forge Welding

added and you should work towards the "drain." By cutting a hole into the cover layers, a flaw in the pattern is unavoidable. Thus you ought to try to get rid of this later on. This can be achieved by positioning the faulty area to the outside again when increasing the number of layers and, if possible, also towards the end of the billet. This way you can finally dispose of it during grinding.

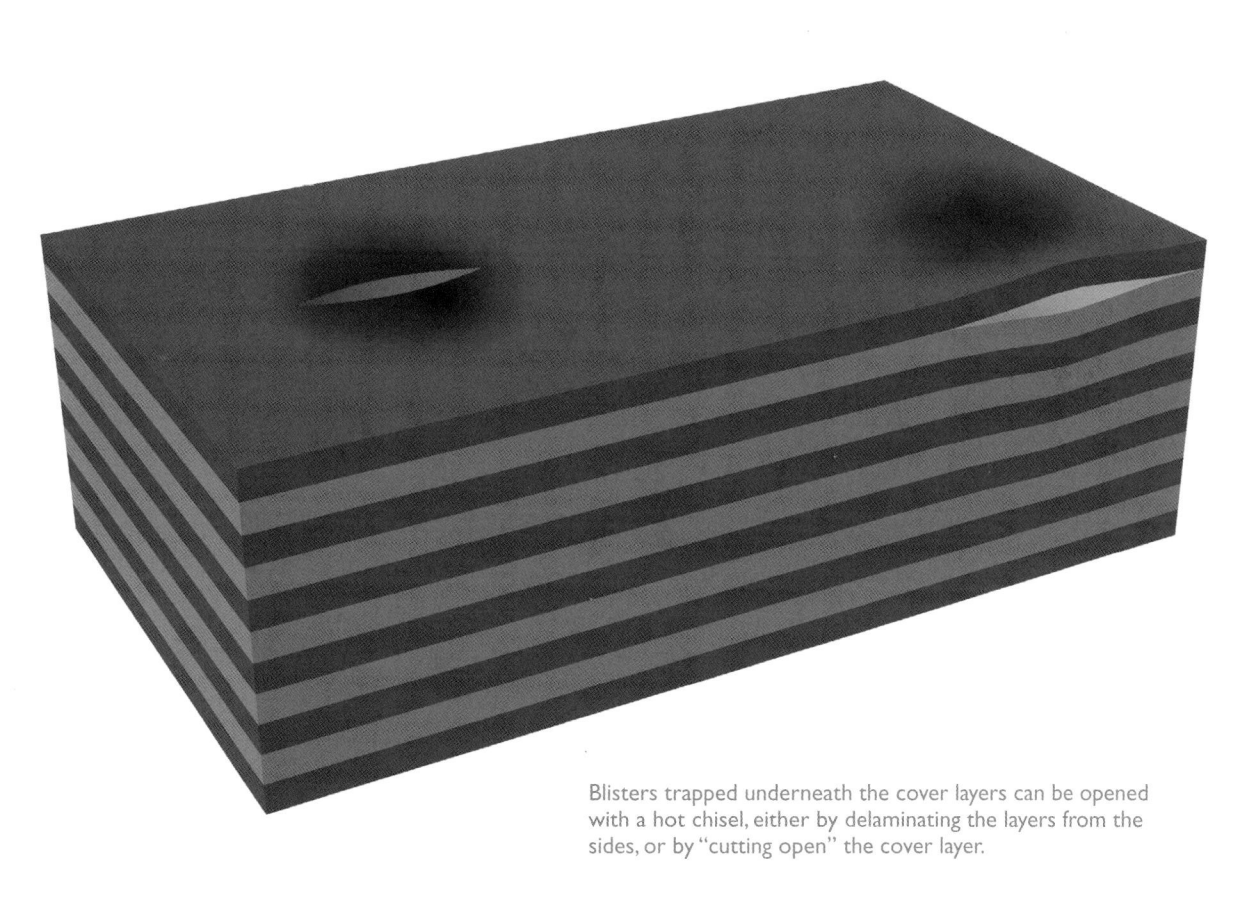

Blisters trapped underneath the cover layers can be opened with a hot chisel, either by delaminating the layers from the sides, or by "cutting open" the cover layer.

Chapter 12: Mosaics

Mosaics

I will explain the various types of mosaic techniques by means of short, practical steps. In chapter 4.2 I already described the basic structure of the individual patterns. As a structure-creating technique, many of the work steps are identical with those for a laminated billet. Differences occur due to the different geometry and order of the parts to be connected, mainly during preparation of the billet.

12.1 Bitmap Mosaic

A bitmap mosaic, as already described in chapter 4.2.1, is created from rods with a square cross-section. These ought to be ground or sandblasted before stacking the billet. Since mixing-up the many different parts can occur easily, it is helpful to mark the faces of one of the steel types (e.g., with a permanent marker). This way the desired pattern can also be checked once more before the start of the actual welding process.

The right angles of the rods ought to be as perfect as possible and their cross-sections should be uniform, otherwise steps and irregularities will be the result. These are especially annoying for strictly geometrical patterns (e.g., chess boards). If the rods are not exactly at right angles, they tend to move apart during later forging and to slant, which makes forge welding more difficult.

To fix the rods, first clamp them into position with two C-clamps and a supplementary piece of flat material that matches the width and height of the billet. After a final check of the bitmap pattern on the marked face, tack weld the rods as usual with an arc welder (see 10.4). For rods with a large cross-section (0.315 inches [8 millimeters] or more), small dots are sufficient to connect the rods together. For thinner rods, it is easier to weld one face completely. The second face surface only has to be tacked on the outside (like a ring surrounding the rods in the center). The handle is best attached to the side which is welded completely. During heating, the billet should always be rotated in 90° steps. Apply flux from all four sides. If possible, the pieces should fit together so tightly that packing (see 11.3) is not necessary. If you can't avoid it, then this process has to be done in two directions.

During forge welding, the billet should also be turned through 90° to achieve a fusion in both directions. Ideally, rotate the billet after each hammer blow around a quarter turn, to and fro.

The individual rods are clamped together with additional pieces of sheet material.

Chapter 12: Mosaics

Since a bit of training is needed to keep time and to always hit vertically, it is easier for beginners to first cover a billet completely with hammer blows from one side, then to turn the billet 90° for the second round. Only light blows should be set to prevent deformation of the billet in the transverse direction.

If the temperature drops too quickly, the billet has to be heated up prior to the second round. In general, welding should be started at the end that is completely welded together and the work should progress towards the "loose" end.

If you feel the welding is complete, add a third and fourth round to be sure, each time turning the billet 90°. As part of the process, the billet ought to be checked for welding flaws (see 11.6). Here, to be on the safe side, two rounds of heating set apart by 90° are recommended. If everything is sound, the billet can be further processed as usual. Since the created image is only visible on the face ends, further steps are usually necessary, like twisting (see chapter 14) or unfolding (chapter 17).

Tip

- Prepare the rods as follows: make sure the surfaces are flat and shiny, place them at 90° angles, square the cross-section according to the measurements of the billet, and mark one type of steel with a permanent marker.

- Clamp the rods together in both directions with C-clamps and an additional piece of flat material. Tack one end face completely, the opposite one only at the outside edges.

- Complete the following work steps from all four sides or from two sides set apart from each other by 90°: heating, adding flux, packing (if necessary), and forge welding.

At one face end all rods are fixated to each other with welding dots and welds.

To prevent the billet from warping during heating due to the different expansion rates of the parts, only the outside edges of the rods are fixed on the opposite end.

Chapter 12: Mosaics

12.2 Spirograph Mosaic

In construction, the spirograph mosaic is similar to the bitmap mosaic, but the square rods are separated from each other by thin steel sheets. For this, the square rods are all of the same steel type (usually a dark one) and the sheet metal in between of a second one.

To assemble the relatively complicated order of materials with the necessary precision, it is helpful to do this layer by layer. This means, you first combine one layer of rods with the small strips of sheet metal. For this, the strips at first can be a bit broader and project somewhat. After tacking, the surfaces of the created layer are again ground flush, thus removing the projecting parts of the dividing sheets.

When the necessary number of layers has been assembled this way, they can be stacked to produce the final billet. In this direction, use thin sheet metal to cover the entire surface and divide the individual layers. If the billet has to be multiplied later on, you can add a covering sheet to one or two sides of steel (separated by 90° from each other) during this work step.

The next steps are identical to the work steps described for the bitmap mosaic. A spirograph mosaic is especially pretty in combination with surface manipulation techniques (see chapter 15).

> **Tip**
>
> - First, tack together one layer of square rods with slightly projecting intermediate sheets.
>
> - Then grind both sides flat.
>
> - Finally, combine several of these layers with intermediate sheets, covering the whole surface to form a billet and tack this as well.

First, the individual "layers," consisting of square rods with sheet metal in between, are put together and fixed.

Chapter 12: Mosaics

Grind off the excess sheet metal on both sides.

Several of the created "layers" are put together to form the final billet and provided with cover layers. These are set apart by 90° in order to multiply the billet later on.

Chapter 12: Mosaics

12.3 Matrix Mosaic

For the matrix mosaic, continuous layers, usually of the same steel type, are combined with individual parts of another steel type lying in between. The latter ones can be wire mesh, individual wires, spheres, powder, or other small parts. The continuous parts create the naming matrix into which the other parts are embedded.

To achieve the creation of a homogenous block free of pores, two issues have to be taken care of during the choice and assembly of the individual parts: First, the continuous layers should at least be as thick as the parts in between. Otherwise problems during welding can show up because inclusions of air or flux will be created. The thicker the continuous layers in relation to the inlaid parts, the smaller this risk, since there is enough material which can be "kneaded" into the gaps.

Second, the inlaid parts have to be arranged in such a way that flux finds a way out of the billet—it is best if this exit is in line with the direction of work (see 11.5). Otherwise inclusions can't be avoided. Because of this, inlaid rings of wire or other closed shapes ought to be avoided. Though the flux is able to move to the inside due to capillary action, it has no possible way of getting out again from the moment the cover layer first fuses with the inlaid ring.

Depending on the kind of parts to be inlaid, it can be problematic to fix them. Quite often it is sufficient to clamp them between the continuous layers and then to tack these. Long wires can be bent in a way that they project from the sides of the billet (e.g., in a wriggly line) to avoid having to fixate many short pieces. The projecting segments are cut off or ground off after forge welding the billet for the first time.

Spheres can be clamped in place securely when both cover layers are provided with a slight depression. It is sufficient to do this on one side. The depressions can be created with a grinding bit or by drilling. For especially difficult cases, like powder or granules, which have to be put between continuous layers, the whole billet can be placed inside a rectangular tube. This technique is described in the section about jigsaw mosaics (12.4). In some cases, the parts can also be fixed by means of spot welding equipment.

Individual wires are fixed on the tiles, here by spot-welding, and placed in the shape of a star.

Chapter 12: Mosaics

Since creating a billet in this way creates many cavities, in most cases compressing or "packing" the billet is decisive for the matrix mosaic. Thus the billet ought to be compressed at normal forging temperature first, to avoid the danger of inclusions. A hydraulic press is optimal for this work step, since it compresses the billet evenly and in an easily controllable way.

If no press is at hand, an especially heavy hammer, or better yet, a power hammer should be used. When the billet is compressed far enough so that there are no visible pores larger than about 0.039 inches (1 millimeter), it is heated to welding temperature while more flux is added. The next steps are identical to working on a typical laminate billet (see chapter 11.4 and the subsequent ones).

For the matrix mosaic, the orientation with respect to the visual surface is decisive for the final appearance of the pattern. Because of this, very unusual patterns can be created by twisting such a billet (chapter 14).

The prepared layers plus a cover layer are clamped together and fixed with welds.

Tip

- Assemble the billet from continuous layers of one steel type, and place inlaid parts of another steel type.

- Inlaid parts should all have the same thickness. Don't use closed ring shapes. Clamp the parts between the layers.

- Packing is best done by means of a hydraulic press; compress the billet until no large pores are visible anymore.

During "packing" with a hydraulic press, the billet is strongly compressed until the open spaces have vanished.

Chapter 12: Mosaics

12.4 Jigsaw Mosaic

With this mosaic variation, as already described in chapter 4.2.4, the possibilities for visual representations in Damascus patterns are refined even more. By using freely shaped parts, you are no longer bound to square pixel rasters.

In principle, most prismatic, semi-finished parts (rectangular and round tubes; L- and T-shapes; round, square, and hexagonal rods; and many more) can be used. In addition, with modern working techniques it is possible to produce (almost) every kind of possible cross-sectional contour. This is especially true when using the technique of Electric Discharge Machining (EDM), which enables you to convert almost any kind of image. In the ideal case, positive and negative parts are created from different steel types, which fit together almost without a gap, like parts of a jigsaw puzzle.

If it is not possible to assemble the billet without remaining cavities, you can fill the gaps with powder, filings, or granules of one steel type as densely as possible. If there is free space on the outside, the billet ought to be framed by a rectangular tube.

To achieve fusion into a solid block, some rules have to be followed during construction of the billet. First of all, it is helpful to give the billet a cross-section that is as close to a square as possible. On one hand, this makes forge welding easier because you can work systematically in two directions (separated by 90°), as already described with respect to bitmap mosaics (12.1). On the other hand, with this method you can easily avoid distorting the image during the forging process.

Since there is no possible way to check the pattern at this stage, your only means of orientation is the proportions of the billet. If a square billet is reduced into a smaller one with a square cross-section by means of forging, the distortion is minimized.

Depending on the contour of the cross-section of the raw materials used, in many cases the flux can't get inside the billet at its longitudinal sides or escape again. You can only try to make do with an addition of flux at the end face, which in turn increases the risk of inclusions because driving out the flux and the detached oxides can only be done in one direction.

Another possibility is to forego the flux entirely, which is only recommended for very tightly packed billets where almost no oxygen can seep in between parts. Then, the billet should be sealed gas-tight all around, including the end faces. To drive out oxygen from small cavities during assembly of the billet, these cavities can be filled with paraffin (candle wax or kerosene). During pyrolysis, when these alkanes burn up, mainly carbon is left over, which doesn't impede welding. Though candle wax has to be warmed up prior to pouring it in, it stays in the billet so this can be stored without problems. If desired, the surrounding tube can be ground off after forge welding.

To tack "open" billets, the same procedure as for bitmap mosaics (see 12.1) is recommended. If cavities located on the inside are to be filled up with powder, first close one end with an arc welder. For larger "channels" use a welded-on piece of sheet metal as a lid. Then fill the cavity with steel powder during several steps—in between them, stamp down with a stick to compress it. Finally, the filler openings should be closed to prevent the powder from trickling out during heating.

For packing and forge welding, the same rules apply as for bitmap mosaics (12.1). For this mosaic variant, the created image only shows up on the end faces. Sections of such billets are often used individually for ornamentations or knife bolsters, or they are put into a carrier layer by means of inlay technique (see 18.3). To make the picture

Chapter 12: Mosaics

visible on the longitudinal side of the billet, further techniques have to be used, like twisting (chapter 14) or unfolding (chapter 17).

> **Tip**
>
> - Prepare the individual parts with clean and shiny surfaces; mark them on the face, if necessary, to avoid mixing them up.
>
> - Assemble the billet, if possible, without gaps; fill the cavities with compressed steel powder or granules. If necessary, frame the billet with a rectangular tube.
>
> - Longitudinally open billet: clamp the billet in both directions with C-clamps and a suitable piece of sheet metal; tack weld one end face completely—tack the other end around the outside edges.
>
> - Assemble longitudinally closed billets in a rectangular tube or framed with sheets of metal, which are welded together gas-tight (with arc welding) along their longitudinal edges. One end face is closed with sheet metal, then powder and/or paraffin is filled in. Finally, the second face is sealed gas-tight with sheet metal.
>
> - Complete the following work steps from all four sides or from two sides set apart from each other by 90°: heating, adding flux, packing (if necessary), and forge welding.

12.5 Mosaics from Finished Parts

As already described in chapter 4.2.5, for this mosaic technique, finished steel parts are used as raw material, which themselves are composed of individual parts. Common variants are made from steel cables or machine chains.

In general, all parts have to be made of steel and should have no kind of coating. Even though the surfaces can only be cleaned to a metallic luster in rare cases, removing as much dirt and residues from lubricants as possible is recommended.

In persistent cases, the parts ought to be put into a solution to remove dirt from hard-to-reach corners. Rust on the surface can be removed by sandblasting, but residue from the sandblasting agent then must be removed from the parts.

12.5.1 Cable Damascus

With steel cables, you have to take care that they are not galvanized and that they are completely made of steel—some cables have a plastic core. These can be used after the core has been removed and replaced by a round steel rod or a thin steel wire. Cables of stainless steel are not suitable because of their high chromium content (for this, see chapter 6.2.3). Since the diameter inevitably becomes smaller during forge welding, a steel cable used as raw material should be as thick as possible (0.78 inches [20 mm] or more in diameter).

Since the individual wires of the cable are usually all the same steel type, no strong contrast can be achieved with this kind of Damascus. Only the welds themselves show up as weak lines. Besides this, the raw materials used for wires are steel types with bad characteristics for tools (e.g., knife blades). They are only optimized for high tensile strength and don't contain enough carbon for a decent heat treatment. Because of

Chapter 12: Mosaics

Prior to working on it, the ends of a steel cable should be secured with electric welding or, as shown here, with binding wire. Photo: Christian Deminie

this, for such applications the material should always be combined with tool steel (suited for the specific purpose): for example, by means of the cover layer technique (see 18.1).

To prepare the billet, a section of the cable (2 to 6 inches [5 to 15 cm] in length) is fused at both ends by arc welding. This prevents the detachment of single strands during heating. Because of the many pores and unconnected parts, heating should be done slowly and by constantly rotating the workpiece. Lots of flux should also be used. To "pack" the steel cable, it is clamped into the vise at one end and then twisted like you are wringing out an old piece of cloth. Thus part of the flux is already driven out. To make this work step easier, using a special tool for twisting is quite helpful (see chapter 14.2).

Forge welding the steel cable has to be done carefully to keep the wires from being driven apart by the transverse thrust of heavy blows. Apart from wires with very large diameters, you should now prefer the handheld hammer over the power hammer because it is easier to control.

Starting at one end, cover the cable spirally with light, overlapping hammer blows which follow the direction of the windings. For this, the workpiece has to be turned constantly, not to and fro as for forging square shapes. One 45° turn (1/8 of a complete rotation) per hammer blow is the rule of thumb. Repeat this process several times and heat the cable to welding temperature again in between, until it is completely covered with blows and has a round cross-section again. After forge welding, the cable is fused into a solid rod with no flexible parts.

Tip

- Use a cable that is not galvanized but made entirely of steel. The diameter should be at least 0.78 inches (20 mm) and work with sections between 2 and 6 inches (5 to 15 cm) in length.

- Clean the cable as much as possible from lubricant residues, dirt, and rust, fuse the ends with an arc welder, and attach the handle as usual.

- Heat the workpiece to welding temperature carefully with constant rotation—add lots of flux.

- For packing, clamp one end in the vise and "wring" it out in the direction of the windings.

- Forge weld spirally in the direction of the windings. Make several runs with light blows until the cable is welded completely and feels stable to the touch.

Chapter 12: Mosaics

12.5.2 Machine Chain Mosaic

As raw material for this variation, all kinds of machine chains can be used: e.g., motorcycle chains, bicycle, and chain saw chains. As already described in chapter 4.2.5, the individual parts are made of different steel types, which leads to a contrast during etching. But this "material conglomerate" is also hardly suited for the creation of knives or other tools because of their non-hardenable contents. Thus, as for cable Damascus, combining these materials with tool steels is recommended—in particular the cover layer technique (see 18.1).

To assure that the billet can be easily worked on, the chain should be folded in a more or less orderly way. For this, it can either be folded into wriggly lines or cut into short pieces which are then put down in parallel. For cutting, the use of an angle grinder (disc grinder) with cutoff wheel is recommended, since sawing is very strenuous because of the hard chain components.

Because of the extremely large cavities in such a billet, its initial size shouldn't be too small in order to achieve a useful size in the end. To create

Chains can be combined to form a billet in different ways. Here is an arrangement of individual sections.

Chapter 12: Mosaics

a reference value, the weight of the chains can be calculated for a solid block (density of steel: 4.5 ounces per cubic inches [7.86 grams per cubic centimeter]).

In general, tacking the chain parts does not pose much of a problem, since the individual welding dots are usually hard to spot in the erratic pattern. To make things easier, the chain strands are arranged lengthwise and are connected at the face ends until the desired width of the billet is achieved. Several of the created layers can be stacked to form a billet and again be tack welded with dots. If the billet by then is still unstable, it can be further stiffened by welding dots along the longitudinal sides. The handle is attached as usual.

Because of the immense porosity of this Damascus variant, ample use of flux and packing are very important. This should be done thoroughly (over the course of several heating cycles, if necessary). To prevent the chain parts from moving apart laterally, it is reasonable to work on two surfaces which are set apart by 90°, as with the bitmap mosaic (see 12.1). Very even and well-controlled packing is possible with a hydraulic press.

When packing this Damascus variant, but also during forge welding, the danger of slag flying around is especially great. The risk of creating large inclusions of air or flux is also especially high. These can blast open explosively during work or while heating up. Because of this, it is necessary to wear protective gear all the time and not only during welding (see 5.2).

After packing, the billet can be forge welded in the usual way, again alternately from two sides separated by 90°. During the design of your project, you should already have in mind that the pattern differs greatly depending on the orientation of the chains (view from the side or from the top). For chains with a more or less "square" cross-section, the single strands can be turned at 90° to each other alternately, which creates a kind of basketweave pattern (see chapter 4.4).

Tip

- Clean as much lubricant residues, dirt, and rust from the chain as possible. Use an angle grinder to cut the chain into pieces appropriate for the length of the billet.

- Put the chain parts next to each other according to the width of the billet and fuse the ends with an arc welder.

- Stack several of these layers to the height of the billet and tack weld them on the end faces. If necessary, set welding dots along the longitudinal sides for stabilizing. Add the handle as usual.

- Complete the following work steps from all four sides or from two sides set apart from each other by 90°: heating, adding flux, packing, and forge welding.

Chapter 13: Multiplication

Multiplication

The structure-influencing technique of multiplication (see chapter 4.4) is used to increase the number of layers for a laminate billet. There are two different methods for this: The classic method is folding. For this, the successfully forge-welded billet is first drawn out to about twice its initial length. Then it is notched in the center with a hot chisel (to about three quarters of the material thickness). After removing the forging scale from the surface (with a wire brush), the front end is folded, so that the billet again has its initial length. After adding flux again, the contact areas can be welded, thus doubling the number of layers. Naturally, by this process the cover layer is fused to "itself," which creates a seemingly thicker layer in the pattern (look also at the remarks in 10.2 for this).

With the second method, stacking, the billet is drawn out to a length which is a multiple of its initial size (three to six times). After this, the work piece is allowed to cool down and the contact areas are freed from forging scale. Now the billet can be cut into several segments, which are stacked like the initial raw materials and connected to a new billet.

As experience shows, the additional effort of every single welding cycle, with respect to stacking, is more than compensated for by means of multiplication. In addition, the probability for flaws declines due to the more careful surface treatment and the smaller number of welding processes (both cause errors). The simultaneous multiplication in two directions, for example from nine square mosaic rods up to a 3 × 3 raster, can only be achieved by stacking.

Folding

Plus
- Material doesn't have to cool down
- Material doesn't have to be freed from forging scale laboriously
- Billet only has to be drawn out a little

Minus
- Since the number of layers is only doubled, many welds are necessary
- By folding, thicker layers are created (disturbing the pattern)

Stacking

Plus
- Due to multiplication, only few welds are necessary
- Maximum flexibility with respect to the arrangement of layers

Minus
- Each cycle is time-consuming (drawing out, allowing to cool, removing forging scale)

Chapter 13: Multiplication

For folding, the billet is notched in the center.

The front part is bent and forging scale is removed from the future contact areas with a wire brush.

Finally, the billet is folded and forging starts again.

Chapter 13: Multiplication

During stacking, the billet is forged out long and then cut into several pieces.

Chapter 13: Multiplication

13.1 Planning

Depending on the thickness of the raw materials and the number of layers you are aiming for, a plan should be made. The main purpose of the plan is to achieve the goal with as few welds as possible.

The number of layers which the object should have in the end depends on aesthetic goal of the project. The "normal" spectrum goes from very few layers (5, 7, 9) up to about 300. With higher numbers, the individual layers are so fine that they hardly create a pronounced pattern, even with a very flat grind. For knife blades with a "fine" pattern, about 100 to 200 layers are recommended.

The examples below ("Calculating Layer Numbers") show different methods for achieving a number of about 120 layers. Here you can see that for folding, all in all five welding rounds are necessary to achieve 112 layers. If the billet instead is drawn out to four times the original length during each cycle and then cut into four pieces accordingly, three welding rounds are sufficient. Additionally, this method also allows for a pattern without irregularities, with respect to the thickness of layers, when an asymmetrical construction of the billet is used (even number of layers, cover layers from different material; see 10.2).

Moreover, if many thin layers are already used as basic material, the result can already be achieved with two welding cycles. The use of an odd number of parts during the last welding has an additional advantage: there is no welding seam in the middle of the billet where the probability for errors is highest because of the lack of thorough heating.

Calculating Layer Numbers

Example 1: Folding

Start: 3 + 4 = 7 layers
1. Welding
Folding: 7 × 2 = 14 layers
2. Welding
Folding: 14 × 2 = 28 layers
3. Welding
Folding: 28 × 2 = 56 layers
4. Welding
Folding: 56 × 2 = 112 layers
5. Welding

Example 2: Stacking

Start: 4 + 4 = 8 layers
1. Welding
Stacking: 8 × 4 = 32 layers
2. Welding
Stacking: 32 × 4 = 128 layers
3. Welding

Example 3: Stacking

Start: 12 + 12 = 24 layers
1. Welding
Stacking: 24 × 5 = 120 layers
2. Welding

Chapter 13: Multiplication

13.2 Drawing Out

Depending on the decision about how many parts the billet should be divided into during each cycle, the length has to be increased by the corresponding multiple. Slight variations don't matter. In the end, it is decisive whether the length of the parts (and thus the length of the billet put together again) is of a size which is easy to work with (see 10.1). The addition of about 0.787 inches (20 millimeters) allows you to cut off the often irregular and slanted ends of the billet.

The billet should not become too broad when it is drawn out. A limit of 1.5 inches (40 millimeters) maximum should not be crossed, if possible. If the billet has to be forged smaller, you should take care to subsequently smooth the surfaces of later contact again. If they stay concave, this easily leads to the inclusion of slag (see 11.7).

Tip

- Forge the billet to a thickness of about 0.787 inches (20 mm) with the layers oriented horizontally, then

- Forge the billet to a width of about 1.18 inches (30 mm) with the layers oriented vertically, then

- Draw the billet to the required length plus 0.787 inches (20 mm) with the layers oriented horizontally.

13.3 Next Steps

As described in chapter 10.3, remove forging scale after the first cycle and each subsequent one with sandblasting. Grinding, especially surface grinding of the contact areas, leads to irregularities in the pattern later on, since the cover layers were removed to a different degree.

An angle grinder is the easiest and best tool for cutting. Here, the use of thin cutting wheels (0.031 to 0.039 inches [0.8 or 1.0 mm]) saves material as well as time. Depending on how "orderly" the ends of the billet look, between 0.196 and 0.59 inches (5 and 15 millimeters) ought to be cut off here.

It makes sense to cut the pieces to the same length as precisely as possible, because otherwise too much material is wasted unnecessarily by projecting layers. If the pieces nevertheless end up having different sizes, it is best to put the longest into the center of the billet.

The new piece, as described in 10.4, can be put together and connected to create a new billet. For this, the contact surfaces, which are coarsest or have the most flaws, should (if possible) be arranged on the outside. For billets with asymmetrical construction, the orientation of the pieces has to be taken into account. The next work steps are identical to the descriptions in chapter 11.

Chapter 14: Twisting

Twisting

By means of this very old technique, amazing patterns can be created without much effort. As a structure-influencing technique, it requires an already welded Damascus billet. This can be a laminate, but for most of the mosaics, twisting also leads to exciting patterns. Besides this, twisting is one method for displaying the front image of a mosaic billet on the longitudinal side. But the motif is distorted and changes depending on the depth of the grind (see 4.5.2).

14.1 Preparation

While twisting a bar, the tensile forces are greatest in the areas farthest away from the center. For this reason, on a billet with a square cross-section, the edges are stretched most. If the billet is twisted too tightly or while being too cold, cracks occur in these areas first.

To minimize this danger, change the billet's cross-section into an octagonal one prior to twisting. But the ends should stay square in order to have a larger contact area for vise jaws and twisting tools (more on this soon). An octagonal cross-section also leads to a "smoother" surface on the completely twisted bar, which lessens the risk of the edges folding over during later forging.

If even and regular twisting is to be achieved, the bar has to be brought to a consistent temperature after the preparations. This is relatively easy with a gas forge or electric oven, but for longer bars and a coal forge this is a real challenge.

If you realize during twisting that the pitch develops in an uneven way, you can correct this trend by partially heating the areas which are less tightly twisted. This can be done easily with an

Demonstration piece by Manfred Sachse. It illustrates the structure of twisted Damascus with several bars.
Photo: German Blade Museum, Solingen, Lutz Hoffmeister

Chapter 14: Twisting

acetylene torch while the billet is clamped in the vise, but can also be done in the coal forge. The billet can also be heated up using the torch from the beginning, but especially for larger diameters, the torch can take a good deal longer than the forge or oven to heat the workpiece.

Tip

- Forge the billet to an octagonal shape, but leave the ends square.

- Heat the bar in the forge as evenly as possible to forging temperature.

Twisting is easier if the bar is first forged to an octagonal cross-section. The ends stay square so that it is easy to clamp and grip the piece.

Chapter 14: Twisting

14.2 Twisting the Bar

To easily twist the bar, clamp one end into a solid (forging) vise. Grip the other end with an (adjustable) tool which, if possible, has symmetrical handles. If using a wrench, the force is applied from one side only and the twisted bar tends to bend, which has to be constantly corrected. A suitable tool would be a large tap wrench (holds screw taps). Even better suited is an adjustable wrench that forms a knee onto which a second handle is welded. An alternative for creating alternating twists (see "maidenhair Damascus" below) is to use three adjustable wrenches with the outer two connected.

Torsion can be varied in many ways, as already described in chapter 4.5. Next to the pitch, which is a result of the number of twists, the direction of twisting can also be determined. The alternating combination of rods twisted in opposite directions is one of the oldest methods with respect to twisting and multiple bar techniques (see 18.2). A rod can also be only partially twisted, separated by straight areas.

The so-called "maidenhair Damascus" is created by changing the twisting direction within a bar. For this, the bar either has to be fixed at two points and twisted by means of a third tool, or it has to be selectively heated bit by bit and twisted in a conventional way: clockwise and anti-clockwise alternately. The latter is easiest if the rod is heated in the forge until heat colors start to appear, then clamped and selectively heated to forging temperature with a welding torch.

Avoid turning an already twisted billet back again because it puts the welds under tension. If the welding wasn't flawless, this may lead to the layers coming apart, which is very hard to correct at this stage.

Tip

- Clamp one side of the bar into the vise and twist the other side evenly with an adjustable wrench with two handles until the desired pitch is reached. If necessary, heat the bar again in between.

- If necessary, selectively heat the bar again with an acetylene torch to correct irregularities.

- Never twist the already twisted bar in reverse!

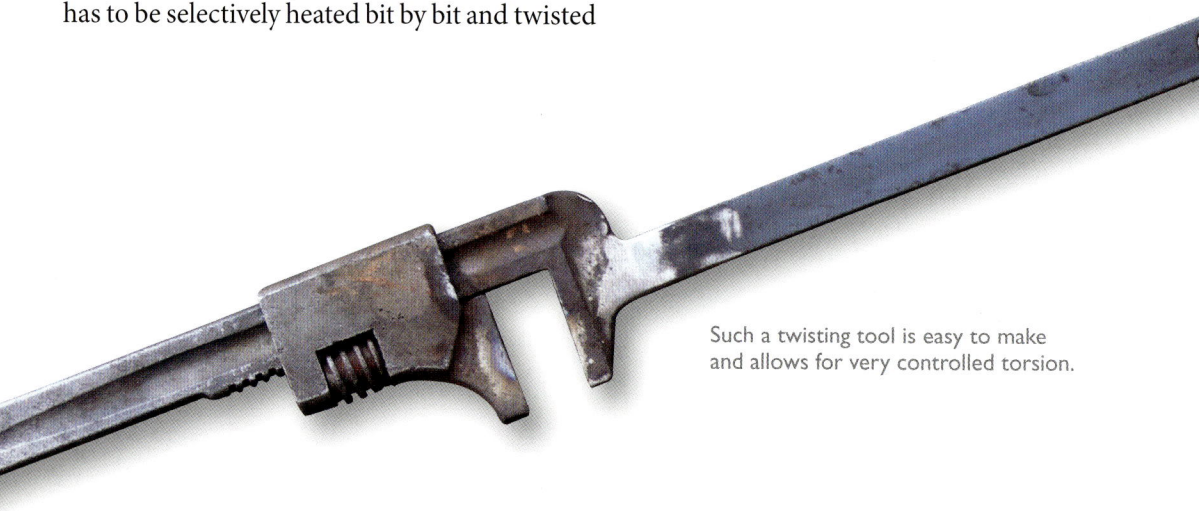

Such a twisting tool is easy to make and allows for very controlled torsion.

Chapter 14: Twisting

The evenly heated rod is twisted steadily until the desired pitch has been achieved.

Chapter 14: Twisting

14.3 Next Steps

When the bar twisting is complete, prior to further forging out, it should be heated to welding temperature and forged once again after adding flux. Thus the welds are stabilized once more and the bar's shape is changed to have a square cross-section. If the cross-section should be kept as large as possible, this can be done by using the spherical dies of a power hammer in a transverse direction (from the center outwards). As described for the bitmap mosaic (see 12.1), here you have to work from two sides set apart by 90°.

Since some of the most interesting grinding states of twisted rods are lying close to the center, the completed billet can be cut apart lengthwise, instead of grinding off much material. For this, an angle grinder with a thin (material saving!) cutting wheel is ideal. Cutting the billet should be done carefully and from all sides to minimize the risk of the cutting wheel jamming in a deep groove. Both halves of the billet can now be used either individually or, for a symmetrical assembly, be turned around and forge welded again "back-to-back."

If several twisted bars are to be combined with the multiple bar technique (see 18.2), they are ground to a metallic luster at the contact surfaces and tack welded at the end faces. To achieve a uniform pattern, you have to make sure that the pitch of the different rods is as homogenous as possible and arranged congruently lengthwise.

Tip

- Heat the twisted bar to welding temperature while adding flux and forge lightly from two sides, set apart by 90°, until the cross-section is approximately square.

- When using a power hammer and spherical dies, forge the rod in a transverse direction.

To achieve a rectangular cross-section, forge the rod in a transverse direction at the welding temperature.

Chapter 14: Twisting

To make the pattern visible in the center without a great loss of material, the billet can be cut open.

Both halves are turned around and welded together, with the former inside located on the outside and with or without a central layer in between.

[Chapter 15: Surface Manipulation]

Surface Manipulation

The structure-influencing technique of surface manipulation in principal is a combination of material removal and deformation with respect to a workpiece. But it is dealt with here separately because it is a classic pattern technique which is applied in many variations. A series of "traditional" patterns which can be created this way can be found in chapter 4.6.

The order of the processes of "material removal" and "deformation" can be varied. The results are comparable to each other, even though there are some differences with respect to details. If the workpiece is first deformed, then ground, it is called embossing; if the order is reversed, the technique is called notching.

As raw material, usually a finely-layered laminate is used. Most mosaics and other structures with characteristic patterns rich in detail don't lead to good results with these techniques. Because of the combination of the various techniques, the patterns become mixed and hard to distinguish.

15.1 Embossing Techniques

With this technique, the laminated billet first becomes structured on the surface by means of embossing at forging temperature. The depth of the embossing should be about 1/4 to 1/3 of the material thickness, if it is done from both sides.

Several methods exist for embossing the workpiece. The simplest is working with the forging hammer: with the hammer peen or a ball-peen hammer, various abstract patterns can be created. But "dents" created this way ought to have a certain depth so enough layers are taken off during the removal of material to create a really pronounced pattern. Working evenly on the workpiece from both sides is very difficult this way.

Larger depressions, made with better accuracy, can be created with various auxiliary tools, embossing hammers, or embossing stamps. This process is very time-consuming since the workpiece has to be heated quite often. The repeated heating without significant deformation furthermore leads to grain growth within the steel, which is especially detrimental to the quality of knife blades and has to be corrected with annealing.

The more practical solution is using a hydraulic press with structured forging dies. The depth and position of the embossing can be controlled very precisely this way. The dies for this can be specially produced, but should be made from hardened tool steel so that it avoids rapid wear at elevated temperatures. As an alternative, you can find parts of machines with suitable shapes (toothed racks, bevel gear wheels, ball-bearing balls, etc.) at the junkyard. You can also use larger, already structured punches from stonemason suppliers.

Another tool, especially suited for serial production, is a structured roll, with which sheet metal can be embossed with an "infinitely" recurring pattern.

When the workpiece has been embossed completely, it is soft annealed (see chapter 19.3), freed from forging scale depending on the object's purpose, and then ground. The most precise and comfortable means for this is a surface grinding machine with a magnetic table. But with a bit of training, the workpiece can also be ground flat with a belt sander (coarse belt, grit P60; see also chapter 19.5). Remove all elevated parts around the embossing until the workpiece is flat again. Another possibility is to face-mill the (well soft annealed!) workpiece.

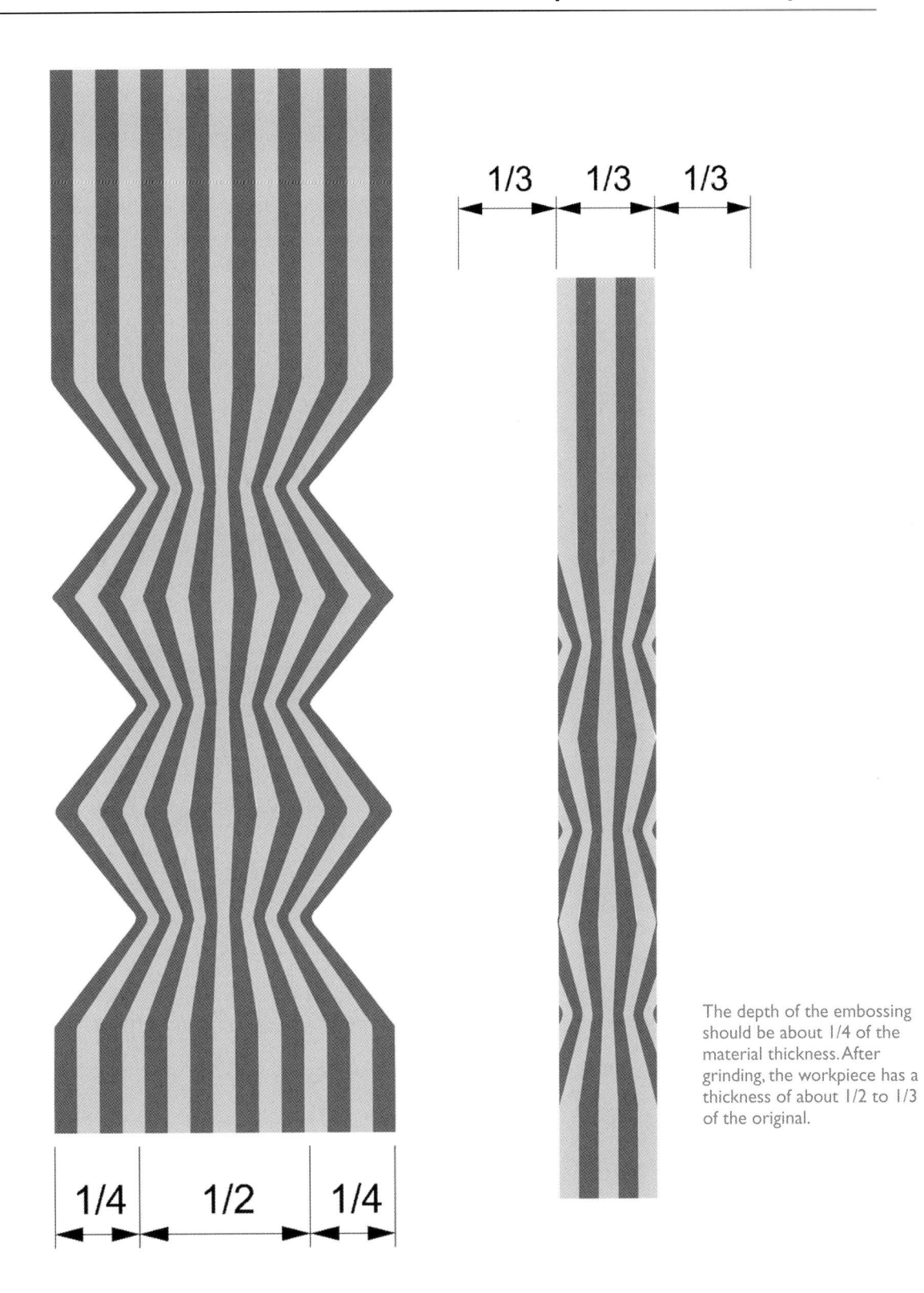

Chapter 15: Surface Manipulation

1/3 1/3 1/3

1/4 1/2 1/4

The depth of the embossing should be about 1/4 of the material thickness. After grinding, the workpiece has a thickness of about 1/2 to 1/3 of the original.

Chapter 15: Surface Manipulation

As an alternative, the object can be ground to its final shape. But here you ought to take into account that the deformation of layers by embossing is weaker towards the center. Thus the pattern becomes more indistinct the more material you remove.

The ground workpiece can also be further processed by means of forging. Here the pattern stays on the surface. It is recommended to forge the object to shape as much as possible and to only grind off a bit of material later on, because the patterns on the surface otherwise become more indistinct. During forging, you have to take into account that the pattern is distorted in accordance with the deformation. This can really disturb geometrical patterns.

Tip

- Heat a fine laminate billet to forging temperature; emboss the pattern with punches and auxiliary tools. It is best to use a hydraulic press and structured dies.

- The depth of embossing should be about 1/4 of the material thickness on both sides.

- Soft anneal the workpiece and remove forging scale.

- Remove the elevated parts by grinding until the workpiece is flat again.

Embossing patterns can also be created with appropriately structured rolls.
Photo: Peter J. Stienen

Demonstration piece showing the embossing technique by Manfred Sachse.
Photo: German Blade Museum, Solingen, Lutz Hoffmeister

Chapter 15: Surface Manipulation

Embossing Technique

Plus
- The pattern doesn't get distorted

Minus
- Various special tools or devices are necessary
- Large material loss

A set of embossing hammers used for creating embossing patterns.
Photo: German Blade Museum, Solingen, Lutz Hoffmeister

Chapter 15: Surface Manipulation

15.2 Notching Technique

With this technique, the desired patterns are first created in the shape of notches by removing material. Here also a notching depth of about 1/4 to 1/3 of the material usually leads to good results. The geometry of the depressions should not have any sharp edges or corners since these enhance the creation of cracks or a "bending over" during forging. Thus you should abstain from creating V-shaped grooves and create a slightly rounded profile. If absolute symmetry isn't mandatory, the patterns can also be slightly shifted with respect to each other when working from both sides. Thus the distortion is minimal when drawing out the workpiece.

If the notches are to be created by means of cutting techniques, the workpiece should be soft annealed prior to this (see 19.3). For only abrasive techniques, you can forego this step under certain circumstances, even though it makes work distinctly easier.

A multitude of machining techniques can be used to notch the material. The oldest and simplest method is filing. Methods supported by machines like drilling, milling, or turning save a lot of time. Depending on the kind of desired pattern, determine the best method and use that. Chapter 19.4 contains some basics with respect to cutting Damascus steel.

For abrasive work, an angle grinder is the obvious tool. Straight notches can be easily created with various cutting and grinding wheels. For delicate and curved patterns a flexible shaft or a rotary tool with various corundum grinding bits can be used.

When the pattern has been notched completely, the workpiece is again heated to forging temperature and flattened again until no depressions are left. The pattern hereby gets distorted (usually in longitudinal direction). The degree of distortion depends on the depth of the notches in relation to the material thickness—the deeper the notches, the more the material has to be drawn out to achieve consistent thickness.

As with the embossing technique, the pattern is rather superficial and becomes less distinct towards the center of the workpiece. Thus the object should be forged to as high a degree as possible and only a little material should be removed by grinding.

Tip

- Soft anneal a fine laminate billet and remove the forging scale.

- Create notches in the shape of the desired pattern by drilling, filing, or with an angle grinder. The depth of the notches should be about 1/4 of the material thickness on both sides.

- Round sharp corners and edges.

- Heat the workpiece to forging temperature and forge it out until the depressions have vanished and a consistent material thickness is achieved.

Notching Technique

Plus
- Rather small loss of material

Minus
- Pattern becomes distorted when forging out

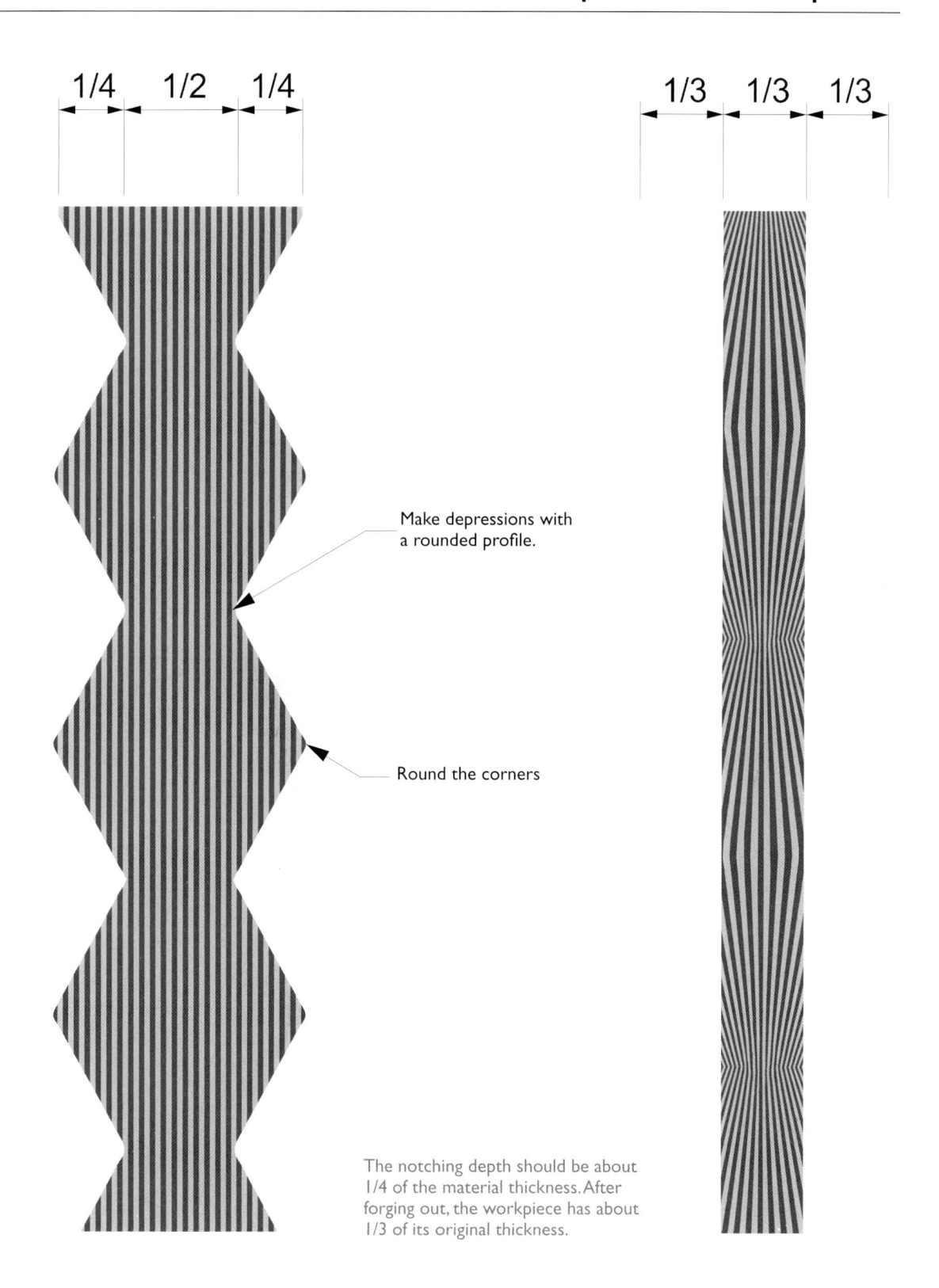

Chapter 15: Surface Manipulation

1/4 1/2 1/4

1/3 1/3 1/3

Make depressions with a rounded profile.

Round the corners

The notching depth should be about 1/4 of the material thickness. After forging out, the workpiece has about 1/3 of its original thickness.

Chapter 15: Surface Manipulation

Straight notches can easily be created with an angle grinder.

The layers cut by the notches are visible on the surface after forging out.

Chapter 15: Surface Manipulation

The created pattern is stretched when the piece is forged flat.

Chapter 16: Deformation

Deformation

Deformation includes all techniques that deform the workpiece and thus the structure of the Damascus. From a technical point of view, twisting is also a deformation technique but is dealt with separately because it is a very common pattern (chapter 14). With forging techniques, various types of deformation can be created. For example:

- Steady or abrupt changes to the cross-section (peaks, widening, steps, etc.)
- Bending
- Compressing
- Crumpling / folding over
- Gaps
- Rolling up

In some cases the deformation can simultaneously be the shaping process for the final object. This has a special appeal with relatively simple patterns, since the Damascus structure follows the shape of the object and thus enhances it (see 3.3.3).

In case further work should follow the deformation, for example with other structure-influencing techniques or as part of a pattern combination (see chapter 18), you should try to achieve a rectangular cross-section to make the subsequent steps easier. However, this is only possible for some of the aforementioned techniques. For others, this is a contradiction. In some cases, by means of combining mirror-inverted, deformed parts a square workpiece can again be put together.

How the deformation is realized really depends on the desired technique and the equipment at hand. In the repertoire of basic forging techniques, many ideas can be found. Thus I don't want to mention any patent remedies, but only offer some basic tips. In general, you should pay attention to the orientation of the already existing Damascus structure. Some types very quickly lead to delaminations of imperfect welds and thus should be avoided, if possible. This is described in chapter 19.1.

If the deforming technique leads to folding over the material, which has to be subsequently forge welded, it is helpful to free coarse forging scale from the contact areas with a steel brush prior to folding (at forging temperature). This makes flux more effective later on.

For a number of deformation techniques a hydraulic press is very useful. With this machine, the workpiece can be really "kneaded." When working with suitable dies, a hydraulic press can also be used for bending and bulging massive workpieces.

16.1 Explosion Pattern Damascus

A widespread variant of deformation techniques is the so-called explosion pattern Damascus. This employs a visual effect which suggests that when the workpiece is being forged out it is deformed differently at the worked areas than in the center of the billet, which distorts the Damascus structure in these areas. For clear and simple patterns this effect is especially pronounced.

To produce explosion pattern Damascus, first you need a laminate billet. It is drawn out with the layers standing vertically and then multiplied by folding or stacking (see chapter 13). Hereby the longitudinal edges of the layers are connected with each other. By means of the superficial deformation, slight offsets are created which make the pattern livelier. For explosion pattern Damascus, folding is preferred over stacking

Chapter 16: Deformation

By deformation, the internal structure of the Damascus becomes distorted and bent.

This cube was deformed by "kneading" with a hydraulic press.

Chapter 16: Deformation

The cube on page 149 forged out to a disc. The folded-over layers are quite visible.

Chapter 16: Deformation

because the repeated deformation created by drawing out enhances the "explosive effect." To achieve a pattern which is as point-symmetrical as possible, the number of layers produced in this way should be equivalent to the number of layers of the original laminate billet. With distorted patterns very interesting effects can be created, too.

To create star-shaped "explosions" or "spiderweb patterns," a laminate billet with asymmetrical structure (i.e., a few bright layers within a mostly dark background) is suited. The billet, as just described, is forged out vertically and folded several times. Finally, the billet is forged at the corners until it again has a square cross-section. Four sections of the billet are rotated 90° to each other, then put together to form a billet and forge welded. This process is technically identical to the one used for bitmap mosaics (see 12.1).

Since the pattern of the explosive pattern Damascus can only be seen on the end faces, further techniques have to be applied, so that it is visible on a longitudinal surface. This, for example, can be done by twisting (chapter 14) or unfolding (chapter 17). Both variants lead to exciting results with respect to explosive pattern Damascus.

Tip

- Forge out a laminate billet with the layers oriented vertically.

- Multiply it by folding or stacking.

- To achieve a star-shaped pattern, forge the billet at the corners until it has a square cross-section again. Arrange four sections of the billet in such a way that a star-shaped pattern is achieved at the face and forge weld again.

- If desired, the pattern can be made visible on a longitudinal surface of the object by means of twisting or unfolding.

Chapter 16: Deformation

Demonstration sequence by Mick Maxen illustrating the production of explosion pattern Damascus. An unsymmetrical laminate billet is welded and, by forging out, deformed with vertically oriented layers.

This billet is forged out into a broader…

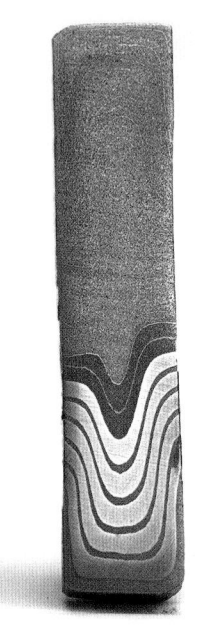

…and a smaller part.

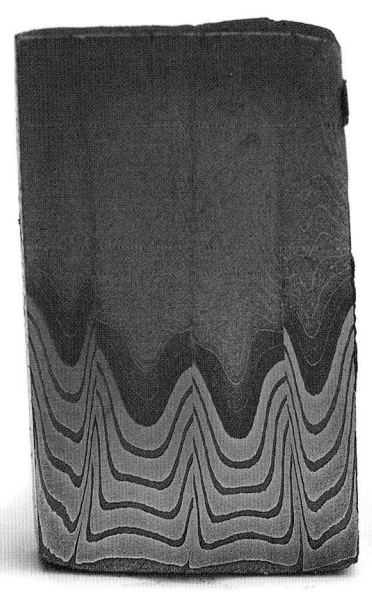

Two pieces each of the smaller and the broader billets are combined; the smaller pieces are located on the outside.

The result is doubled by folding…

Chapter 16: Deformation

…and doubled once more.

Now the billet is forged "at the corners" until a square cross-section has been achieved again. The original pattern now appears to be turned 45°.

Finally, four sections of this billet are combined to form a star-shaped explosion.

Chapter 17: Unfolding

Unfolding

When creating many interesting Damascus patterns, especially image-like mosaics and inscriptions, at first they are only visible on the face ends of the billet. To make them visible on the longitudinal surface of an object (e.g., a knife blade), slices of such a billet can be put onto a core layer similar to tiles (see chapter 18.1). This strenuous and time-consuming process can be simplified by means of the unfolding technique.

Here the billet is notched alternately on opposite sides, then unfolded like an accordion and drawn out until it again has a consistent material thickness and plane surfaces. By unfolding, mirror-inverted patterns of the initial motif are created, which can be used as an element of design.

Notching, which in earlier times was done by means of a hot chisel, can be simplified significantly by using an angle grinder with a thin cutting wheel. The depth of the notches should be chosen in such a way that the remaining material thickness is about the same as the thickness of the individual "slices." At most this should be about one third of the billet's width.

The bottom of the indentation should be as round as possible (which is automatically achieved when using a cutting wheel) to minimize the risk of cracks during unfolding. To avoid having the edges next to the indentations folded over during forging out, you can slightly round them.

The completely notched billet is now heated to welding temperature and unfolded piecewise. Hereby it is recommended to first open all the notches with an anvil chisel, then to bend them open one by one with slight hammer blows at the edge of the anvil. Since tensile forces can be high at the bottom of the notches and cracks, and detachment of layers can easily occur, bending open has to be done carefully and under no circumstances at too low a temperature.

After the billet has been unfolded to form a "straight" bar in this way, it again is heated to welding temperature and drawn out lengthwise until the "nodes" of the bends are level.

Tip

- Notch the billet to be unfolded from both sides alternately with an angle grinder equipped with a thin cutting wheel.

- The remaining material thickness is equivalent to the distance between two opposite indentations (at most a third of the billet's width).

- Heat the billet to welding temperature and open all indentations with an anvil chisel, then bend them open at the anvil's edge at high forging temperature.

- Draw out the "wriggly-line billet" at welding temperature until the bends are level.

Chapter 17: Unfolding

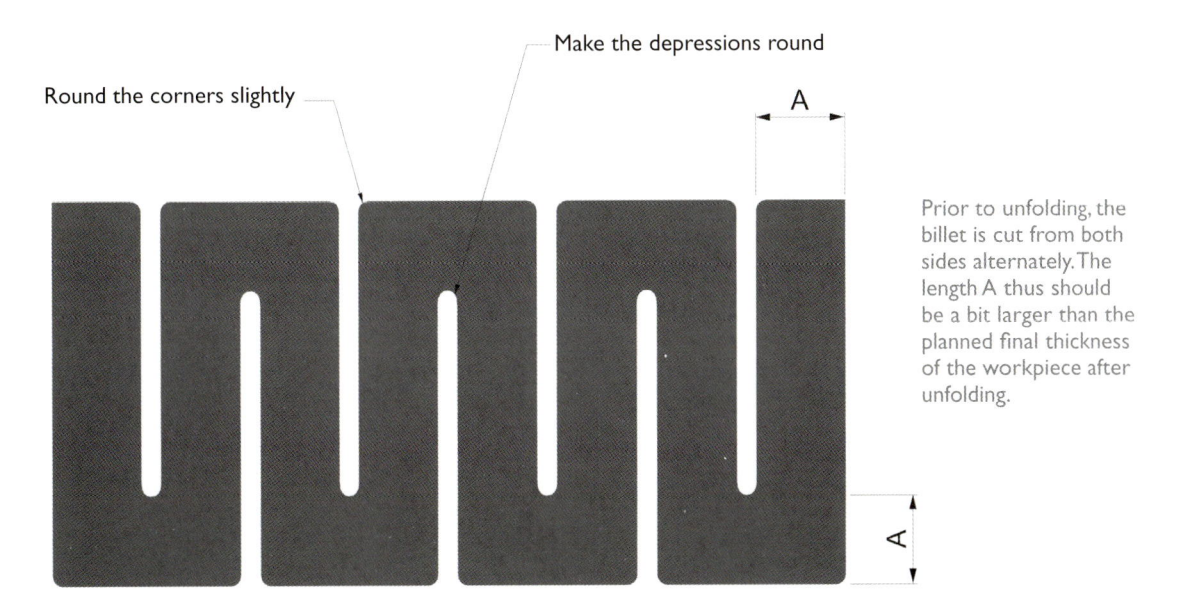

Round the corners slightly

Make the depressions round

A

Prior to unfolding, the billet is cut from both sides alternately. The length A thus should be a bit larger than the planned final thickness of the workpiece after unfolding.

A

Demonstration piece by Peter J. Stienen illustrates the unfolding technique.
Photo: Peter J. Stienen

Chapter 18: Pattern Combinations

Pattern Combinations

In many cases, individually created or separately treated Damascus structures are combined. Depending on the orientation of the individual components in relation to the visual surface, this can be done with a cover layer technique or with the multiple bar technique. An additional possibility is partial inlays.

18.1 Cover Layer Technique

For this technique a core layer, which in many cases consists of a monosteel, is covered with a patterned Damascus. The procedure is similar to veneering wood panels.

In principle, such a three-layer construction is treated like a laminate billet. Core layers and cover layers are put together in the desired arrangement and tack welded at the face ends. The relation of material thicknesses of cover layers and core layer is kept during drawing out, which has to be taken into account with respect to further treatment. If a blade is ground from the material, the cover layer is partially removed and the layer for the blade edge thus revealed. The thicker the edge layer is in relation to the cover layers, the broader it is revealed by grinding. A very thin core layer, however, can easily be off-center if the blade wasn't forged very conscientiously and straight. This is especially unfavorable if non-hardenable materials like nickel were used for the cover layers.

Besides cover layers covering the whole surface, individual "tiles" (e.g., cut-off slices of a mosaic billet) can be attached to the core layer. The pieces ought to be put next to each other as closely as possible they should not show any gaps. For fixing the pieces it is easiest to put the smallest possible tacking dots to the corners of the tiles at the longitudinal sides, which will be removed by grinding after the forge welding. It is not possible to fix more than two rows of tiles this way. But under certain circumstances this may also be done with dot-welding equipment.

18.2 Multiple Bar Technique

For this technique, several Damascus bars with more or less square cross-sections are combined. They lie next to each other, parallel to the later visible surface of the object.

The individual components ought to be shiny at the contact areas and, if possible, ground flat. Here it is important that the cross-sections of the individual bars stay at right angles. Now the bars are put together in the planned order and tacked at the face ends. A small, high billet is the result, which can lead to problems during forge welding. The more bars are combined, the higher the billet becomes in relation to its width. This unfavorable ratio easily leads to the billet tilting and the bars being driven apart laterally with a hammer blow that is not set exactly straight. Thus you have to work very carefully and conscientiously to put the billet down exactly upright and to work on it with well-placed, straight hammer blows.

If the billet becomes tilted or bulges to one side, it is extremely difficult to save it. In some cases, the only fix is to let the billet cool down and then separate the individual bars from each other, making the contact areas right angles and parallel again by grinding. But part of the pattern is lost this way.

If the welding was successful, the multiple bar billet can be treated further as usual. Exactly like the similarly constructed striped Damascus (see 4.3), a multiple-bar billet shows the development of the structure very well with clear changes to

Chapter 18: Pattern Combinations

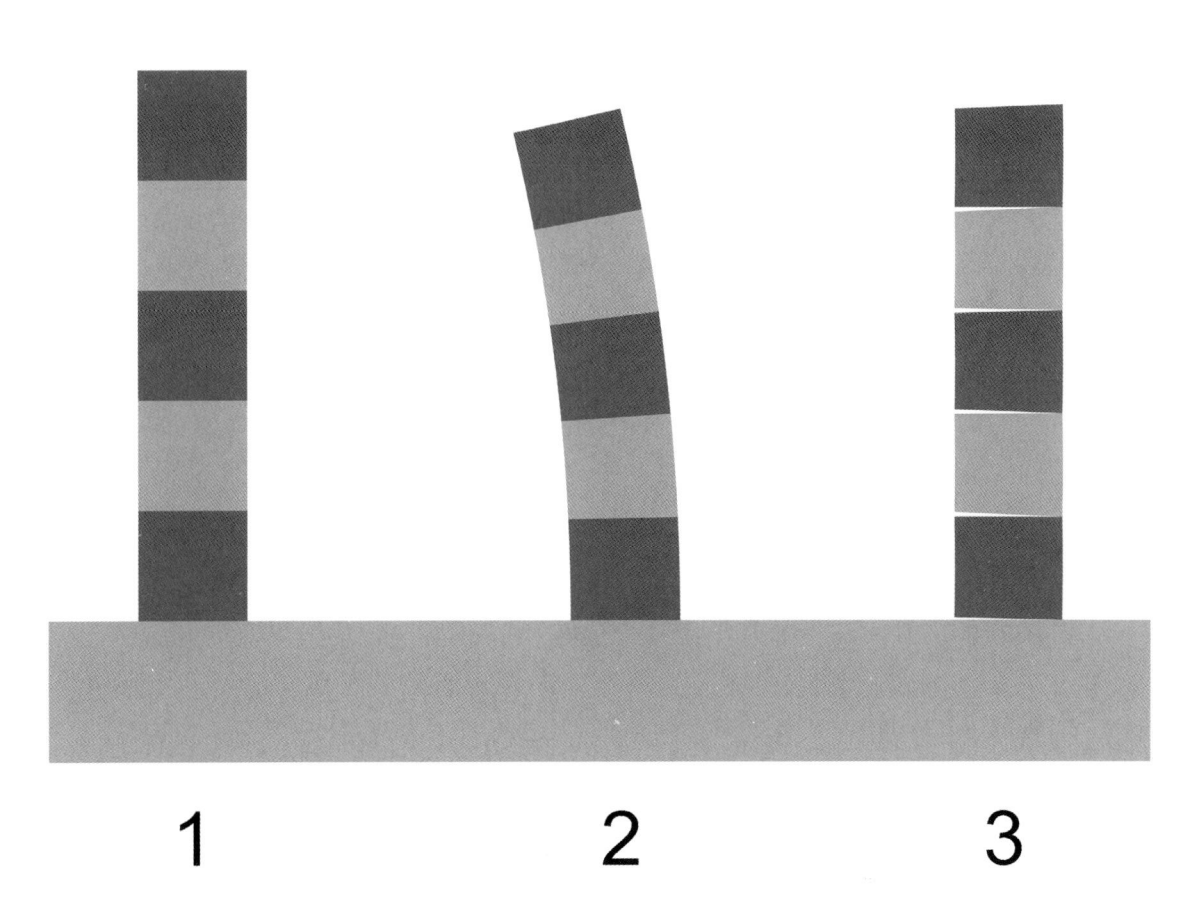

1 **2** **3**

Because of the unfavorable relation of height to width in the multiple-bar billet, it reacts sensitively to tilted hammer blows. When it is already deformed (2), it is very hard to rescue because after correcting, the individual bars no longer have full contact (3), and thus easily "break away" to one side.

the cross-section. If desired, the contour of the final object can be rough forged to underline this effect.

A classic multiple-bar structure uses several rods alternately twisted to the right and left with the same pitch. If such an arrangement is ground as a knife blade, a sequence of different grinding states is displayed (see 4.5.2), since more and more material is removed from the rods to shape the blade edge.

18.3 Inlay Technique

Instead of fully covering a core layer with "tiles" of another Damascus type, single elements can be inlaid into a surface. The lateral surfaces of the inlay should be slanted towards the underside (about 45°), if possible, and the lower edges should be rounded. Vertical surfaces lead to a mostly lateral displacement of the basic material, thus creating gaps around the small, inlaid plates, which are difficult to close again.

Chapter 18: Pattern Combinations

The used inlays should have as small a material thickness as possible to avoid displacing much of the basic material to achieve a plane surface again. Thick parts can be inlaid in prepared depressions, which means more effort with respect to preparation. These kinds of depressions can be created by embossing, for example, using a hydraulic press and the (cold) plates to be inlaid. Material-removing techniques (milling, drilling, etc.) are also possible. The lateral faces of the depression have to be slanted, too, to avoid inclusions of slag and flux.

The depth of the depressions has to be chosen in such a way that the tiles still project about 0.078 to 0.118 inches (2 to 3 millimeters). This way they will be pressed into the basic material by the welding hammer blows and fusion will be achieved over the entire area. In addition, the tiles should project somewhat laterally (0.039 to 0.078 inches [1 to 2 millimeters]). Embossed depressions should be freed from forging scale by sandblasting prior to inserting the small plates.

In many cases, fixing the parts on the basic material is a problem. Depending on the situation, they can perhaps be secured with small tacking dots, which later are covered by the projecting border of the inlay. Spot welding equipment can also serve well here. In a pinch, you can also use binding wire, which is removed after the first welding blows. To avoid fusion between wire and Damascus billet, stainless steel wire (containing chromium) ought to be used.

While forge welding you have to add ample flux. The welding blows have to hit the center of the tiles first and then be continued towards the borders to drive out flux and oxides. Finally, the borders of the small plates are fused with the basic material.

In general, linear elements can also be inlaid, as is the case for wire damascening, for example (see 4.10). For this, corresponding grooves have to be prepared, which can be done by means of a cutting wheel or a small high speed steel (HSS) spherical cutter. With this method, too, the inlaid parts should project in height as well as laterally so they can be pressed into the basic material.

Since inlays are superficial patterns, the object should be largely forged to shape already and only be ground somewhat afterwards to avoid removing the meticulously inlaid decorations again.

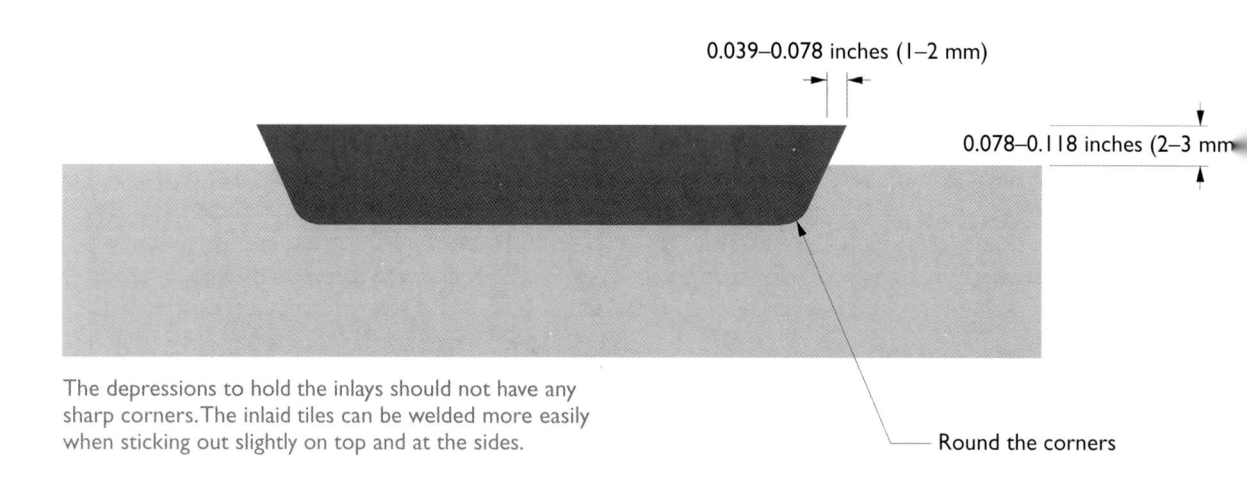

0.039–0.078 inches (1–2 mm)

0.078–0.118 inches (2–3 mm)

The depressions to hold the inlays should not have any sharp corners. The inlaid tiles can be welded more easily when sticking out slightly on top and at the sides.

Round the corners

Chapter 19: Working with Damascus

Working with Damascus

In this chapter I will deal with the characteristic features of working with forge-welded Damascus using various techniques. I hope the reader finds helpful tips here.

19.1 Forging

When forging forge-welded Damascus you have to realize, above all, that the welds in most cases are weak spots of the material. A combination of tensile and shear stress (peel stress) leading to a detachment of layers is especially unfavorable, but only happens in special cases.

Usually the most detrimental stress is created during the broadening of material with vertically oriented layers. This places the welds under tensile stress. Depending on circumstances, peel stress can also be created by mushrooming of the workpiece.

In general, you ought to avoid such expansion: for example, by starting with an appropriately high billet, which is forged to be more narrow. If the process is unavoidable, the ends of the billet can be held together by a weld done with the arc welder, which is removed again in the end. The expansion should be done very carefully and only at very high temperatures.

Forging processes in which the welds only experience compressive loads usually don't pose special problems. But when using materials with high carbon content, you have to take care that the forging temperature is kept within the correct range to avoid the creation of cracks.

If delamination of individual parts occurs during forging, the fault has to be corrected immediately by further forging to avoid an exacerbation of the problem.

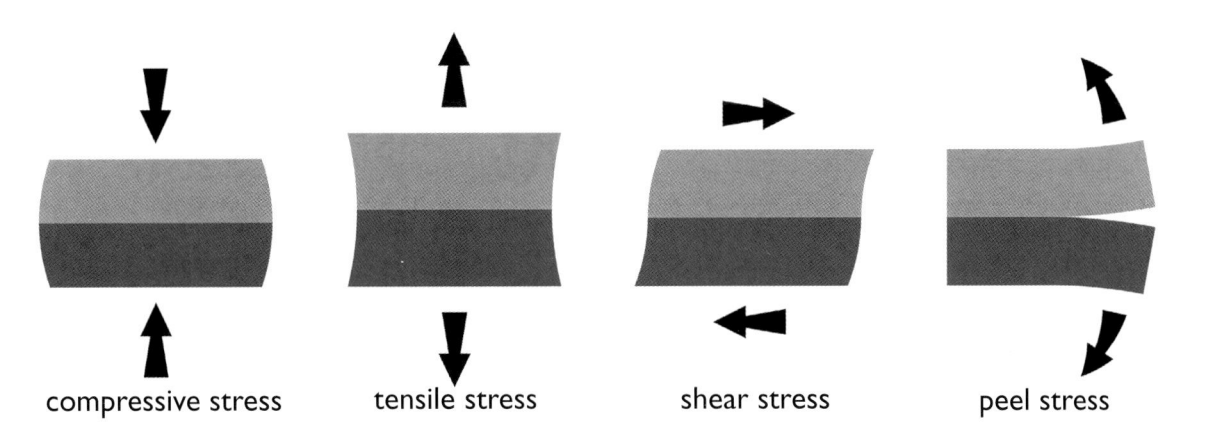

compressive stress | tensile stress | shear stress | peel stress

Compressive loads on welds don't pose any problem. Tensile loads and shear stress are more problematic, but can be compensated for by working carefully.

Chapter 19: Working with Damascus

> **Tip**
>
> - Peel and tensile loads on the welds should be avoided, if possible, or kept small.
>
> - If these can't be avoided, the ends of the billet should be secured by a weld made with an arc welder and removed later on.

19.2 Cutting

Besides the forging method of splitting, most of the abrasive and thermal cutting methods can be used, too. It is not recommended to use a cold chisel or shearing. All of the introduced methods work in a hard or soft annealed state as well, with slight limitations for abrasive cutting (more wear and tear on the tools).

The most effective manual method is using an angle grinder with a thin cutting wheel (0.031 or 0.039 inches [0.8 or 1.0 mm]). The thin wheel reduces the loss of material and the introduction of heat to the workpiece. The latter is of importance if the workpiece was already soft annealed prior to cutting. Through intense heating the material tends to harden around the cut edge, which makes later machining work more difficult. This problem is most significant for cutting thin cross-sections.

If necessary, with curved cuts the material can also be cut by means of an acetylene cutting torch or plasma arc cutter. Here you have to take into account that the various steels get melted down in the area of the cut edges, and this material has to be removed to once again reveal the Damascus structure. Besides this, strong hardening takes place at the cut edges.

Laser or water jet cutting methods also work well and without limitations. Because of the material's tendency to corrode, working with the laser usually is the better choice. Here, too, the cut ends harden, but much less so than with torch cutting. When using more targeted energy sources, like laser cutting, melting the layers is normally so limited that this area is removed with further surface treatment.

> **Tip**
>
> - Manual cutting tools include: angle grinder with thin cutting wheel (0.031 or 0.039 inches [0.8 or 1.0 mm])
>
> - Mechanical: laser jet cutting

Laser cutting enables precise cutting of the contour. The material doesn't have to be soft annealed.

Chapter 19: Working with Damascus

19.3 Soft Annealing

When the forging is completed, the material should be soft annealed prior to any machining or abrasive work. Typically Damascus steel objects have rather thin cross-sections, and some of the materials used to make the steel tend to partially harden while cooling down in a normal atmosphere. This makes the abrasive work more difficult and also wears out grinding belts very fast. Machining such workpieces is often torturous and only possible with carbide metal tools.

An easy method for soft annealing is to let the workpiece cool down within the slowly cooling embers of the coal forge. But this method is not especially recommended because the results are not consistent.

With an electric oven, on the contrary, very good results can be achieved. For this, the workpiece is heated to a certain temperature (for most raw materials and their combinations, the range is 1,260°F to 1,290°F [680 to 700°C]; see table 01 in the appendix). This has to be held for a certain time (depending on the cross-section, about 45 to 60 minutes). After this, the oven can be switched off so the workpiece can cool down over a long time. Depending on the insulation of the oven, this can take between four and twelve hours.

Such a holder can easily be made of sheet metal and is practical for any kind of heat treatment in the oven.

Chapter 19: Working with Damascus

To protect the tools during further work, remove the layer of forging scale with a sandblaster after soft annealing.

An overview with data for heat treatment of the materials introduced in chapter 6.3 can be found as a table in the appendix of the book (on page 171).

Tip

- Heat the workpiece in the electric oven to about 1,290°F (700°C).

- Leave it there for 60 minutes.

- Switch off the oven and let the workpiece cool down without opening the oven.

- Remove the forging scales from the workpiece (sandblasting).

Soft annealing blades in an electric oven.

Chapter 19: Working with Damascus

19.4 Machining

As long as the material has been soft annealed, machining work on Damascus steel has no special requirements. This is valid for filing, sawing, drilling, turning, milling, and other kinds of machining methods. Tools, cutting speed, and coolant have to be chosen depending on the material. Since the raw materials of Damascus steel are most often tool steels, HSS tools are effective and long-lasting. Depending on cost, carbide metal tools (e.g., carbide cutting inserts) are highly recommended.

For relatively coarse patterns and materials with large variations in composition, a loss of surface quality may be the result of the different effects of machining, which means that the workpiece has to be ground once more afterwards. For very strict specifications for the dimensions (fit), this has to be taken into account beforehand.

If it is necessary to further work on an already hardened workpiece, this can only be done by means of carbide metal tools. Tools completely made from carbide metal (drill bits, cutting bits, reamers, etc.) are extremely expensive and can also break easily. As a cheaper, but not quite as effective, alternative you can convert a drill bit for concrete which has a (blunt) plate of carbide metal in its tip. By sharpening the bit appropriately, you can use it for working with steel.

Tip

- Soft-anneal the material well!

- Use HSS or, if affordable, carbide metal tools. Use files of good quality; the others wear out all too soon.

- Choose the cutting speed, coolant/lubricant, etc. in accordance with the materials used in the steel. If in doubt, concentrate on the steel with the highest carbon content.

Various machining tools (left to right): reamer, twist drill bit, face mill, screw taps, and various milling cutters.

Chapter 19: Working with Damascus

19.5 Grinding

Working with various grinding techniques usually takes up a majority of the time spent on producing an object made from Damascus steel. Thus, this lengthy work should be optimized any way possible. This can be achieved with optimal soft annealing and high quality grinding materials and corresponding machines. Experience shows that by taking small steps between the different grits used, the working time and the amount of grinding material can be lessened. This is especially true for the precision work done after hardening.

A universally proven auxiliary device is the belt sander. When purchasing a belt sander you ought to take care that grinding can be done at the contact wheel as well as the flat surface. The length of the belt, if possible, should not be below two meters because the shorter the belt, the quicker the workpiece heats up. If possible, the belts should have no overlapping glue joint. Speed control for the machine makes sense because for finer grits, lower speeds lead to better results.

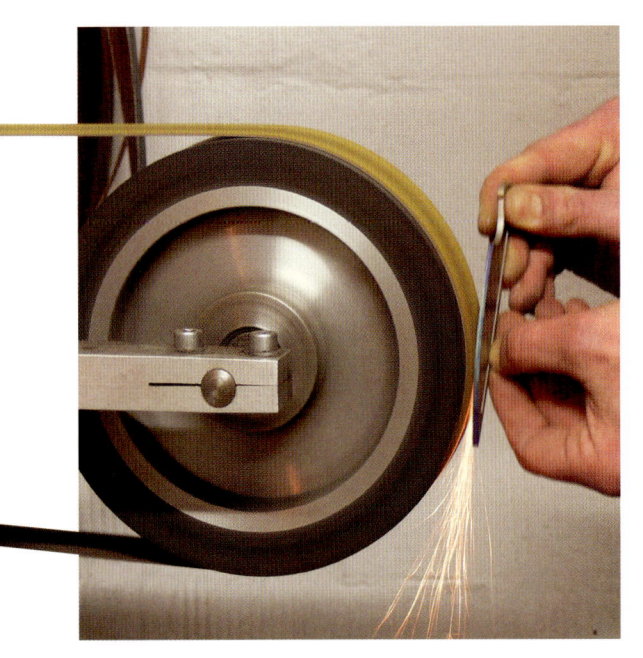

The belt sander is a universal tool for working on Damascus.

There is no patent remedy for working out small, difficult-to-access radii and corners. Small grinding wheels, corundum grinding bits, flap wheels, sanding bands mounted on rubber arbors, or similar auxiliaries can provide a solution here. A large variety of tools used for goldsmithing can be used for working with steel as well. Often the best solution is the combination of these tools with various methods of manual grinding.

Since, after hardening, overheating the material has to be avoided at all cost, working with machines should only be done at low speed and with great care, especially when working at the thin cutting area of a blade after hardening. It is mandatory to use coolants whenever using machines. A grinding stone cooled with water is quite effective. Besides grinding and polishing a knife edge, a grinding stone can also be used for fine-grinding the surfaces of other objects.

Nevertheless, you won't get around grinding some spots manually. Here, investing in the best material available pays off, because even this gets blunt quickly enough. In any case, you should use abrasive cloth, if available, at the needed grit size. You can easily tear it into suitable pieces to fit snugly around sanding blocks and in tight corners: also, it has a longer life than sandpaper. Very fine grits (above P400) are only rarely available in abrasive cloth. For this purpose, lapping and honing films with grit sizes of 30 µm and smaller are an excellent alternative. The life expectancy of these consumable materials, especially for fine grits, can be prolonged by using oil.

For very fine polishing and the intermediate grinding between etching (see 19.7), so-called Micro-Mesh abrasives have proven effective. They have a good service life and are available in extremely fine grit sizes. (Buyer beware: the Micro-Mesh sizes don't relate to the familiar

Chapter 19: Working with Damascus

grading system. The finest grit, MM12,000, corresponds to P4,000, approximately).

Here are some recommendations for the order of various grinding processes and the tools used:

Soft annealing / Sandblasting

a) Grinding to shape
   Belt sander P60 / filing / manual grinding P80
b) Fine grinding
   Belt sander P120 / manual grinding P120

Hardening /Sandblasting / Annealing

c) Leveling out warping (be very careful of overheating!) Wet grinding stone P240 / belt sander P120 / manual grinding P120
d) Fine grinding
   Belt sander P400–P600 /
   manual grinding P220–P320–P400
e) Finish
   Wet grinding stone P800 / manual polish P600–P800

Etching

f) Intermediate polish / shading
   Manual polish P1,200–P2,000
   (MM3,600–MM6,000–MM12,000)

Various tools for manual grinding (left to right): a holder for abrasive cloth (covered with rubber on one side), lapping and honing films, abrasive cloth, Micro-Mesh pads.

Grinding tools for machines (left to right): holder with abrasive sleeve, silicone polishing wheel, flap wheel, corundum grinding bits, and diamond wheel.

Chapter 19: Working with Damascus

19.6 Hardening & Annealing

The heat treatment of steel is an art. To deal with this topic in depth would be too much within the framework of this chapter. As already done in earlier chapters, I again want to refer to the book *Knife Blades and Steel* (*Messerklingen und Stahl*) by Roman Landes. In the following, I'll only give some tips. However, without a thorough understanding of the hardening process, these tips are not sufficient to achieve goals in specific cases and with special characteristics.

Besides its influence on the mechanical properties of the material, its structure also affects its reactivity with different etching media. A hardened workpiece is corroded by acids noticeably more than a soft annealed one, and its contrast is also more striking. This means that a Damascus object should always be hardened if a strong contrast is desired. In fact, partial hardening should be avoided because the etching will not be uniform.

For hardening, the workpiece first has to be heated, then quenched. The temperature to be achieved, the holding time, and the kind of quenching medium are dependent on the materials used and the cross-section of the workpiece—this can be looked up in steel tables. A tried and tested method is to use the highest of the hardening temperatures and the softest of the quenching media for a combination of different materials. If no decent hardness is created, another attempt can be made with a "stronger" quenching medium.

The holding time mostly depends on the cross-section of the workpiece. You can almost neglect it for knife blades. Two to five minutes is sufficient (for low-alloy steels). An unnecessarily long holding time leads to undesired grain growth, which in turn is negative for the quality of a knife edge.

After the workpiece has been heated evenly to hardening temperature, it is cautiously removed from the oven and quenched. To avoid, or at least minimize, warping, the workpiece ought to be submerged rapidly and evenly into the quenching medium, then slowly moved to and fro. After a certain amount of time (depending on the cross-section), it is cold enough and can be removed.

For annealing most tool steels, a simple kitchen oven is sufficient.

After quenching and cooling, it is recommended to thoroughly remove possible oil residues. Forging scale and dirt can be removed with a sandblaster before the precision work is started.

Annealing should be done within four to six hours after hardening, if possible. A common, commercially available kitchen oven is well-suited for this. Annealing usually is done in two or three cycles, which means the workpiece is heated several times and held at temperature for a certain amount of time. Between the cycles, it is removed from the oven and allowed to cool down. The temperatures and holding times depend on the materials and the planned use of the object. Here are recommendations for heat treatment, which work for the following material combinations:

- O2 + 1.2767 (similar to L6 / 1.2713)
- O2 + 15N20
- O2 + nickel

Hardening: 1,510°–1,545°F (820–840°C), Holding time 2–20 min

Annealing: 360°–430°F (180–220°C), holding time 2 x 45–60 min

An overview with data for heat treatment of the materials introduced in chapter 6.3 can be found in the table in the appendix.

19.7 Etching

The various etching media and their qualities were already introduced in chapter 9.2. How long (i.e., how deep) the Damascus ought to be etched strongly depends on the vision for the material's design. To only make the pattern visible, a very brief etching is sufficient. The advantage of this is that the "bright" steel hardly tarnishes, and thus a very pronounced contrast and crisp borders between bright and dark can be achieved.

With longer etching duration the bright steel becomes darker, too; the borders are less pronounced and a relief is created. This allows the possibility to make the bright parts completely shiny again by intermediate polishing. This should only be done with very fine grits (P1200 and more) and under running water.

Hereby you should apply almost no pressure, so you don't brighten the deeper lying parts as well. With several short etching rounds and intermediate polishing using increasingly finer grits, shades can be created that provide additional plasticity to the pattern.

The object ought to be hardened and finely polished (minimum P800) prior to etching. Execute the finishing steps very carefully, since—especially with coarse patterns—every trace of grinding that isn't removed becomes visible during etching.

To achieve a consistent and even etching, all grease and fat has to be thoroughly removed from the object. This can be done by means of spirit, acetone, or precipitated chalk, but common dish soap is also very effective. To keep oils from your hands off of the workpiece, wear rubber gloves (which, of course, have to be free of oil on their outside as well!). After the object has been cleaned under running water with a sponge and ample dish soap, all residues from the detergent (and also the gloves) must be washed off—they cause irregularities when etching.

If sulfuric or citric acid is used, these can be heated in the water bath to about 120°F (50°C) to shorten the etching time. This isn't necessary for $FeCl_3$. If the acid is heated, it ought to be inside a glass receptacle; otherwise acid-resistant plastic can be used. It makes sense to choose the receptacle depending on the geometry of the object so that complete submersion is possible without using too much acid. For blade edges, a graduated cylinder from a laboratory supplier works well. They are available in various sizes and made of glass or plastics. To submerge the object and pull it out later on, it can be attached to a stainless steel wire. Because an inconsistent

Chapter 19: Working with Damascus

> ## Tip
>
> ### Etching with FeCl$_3$
>
> - Clean all oils from the workpiece thoroughly with dish soap; rinse.
> - Submerge in FeCl$_3$; check the etching; rub with steel wool, if necessary; remove fat again; rinse; repeat the test.
> - Etch for 5 minutes, then rub off the black coating.
> - Etch for 10 minutes.
> - Intermediate polish with MM3600
> - Etch for 5 minutes.
> - Intermediate polish with MM6000.
> - Etch for 5 minutes.
> - Finish with MM12000.
> - Rub with oil.
>
> The etching times depend on the concentration of the acid—try it out!

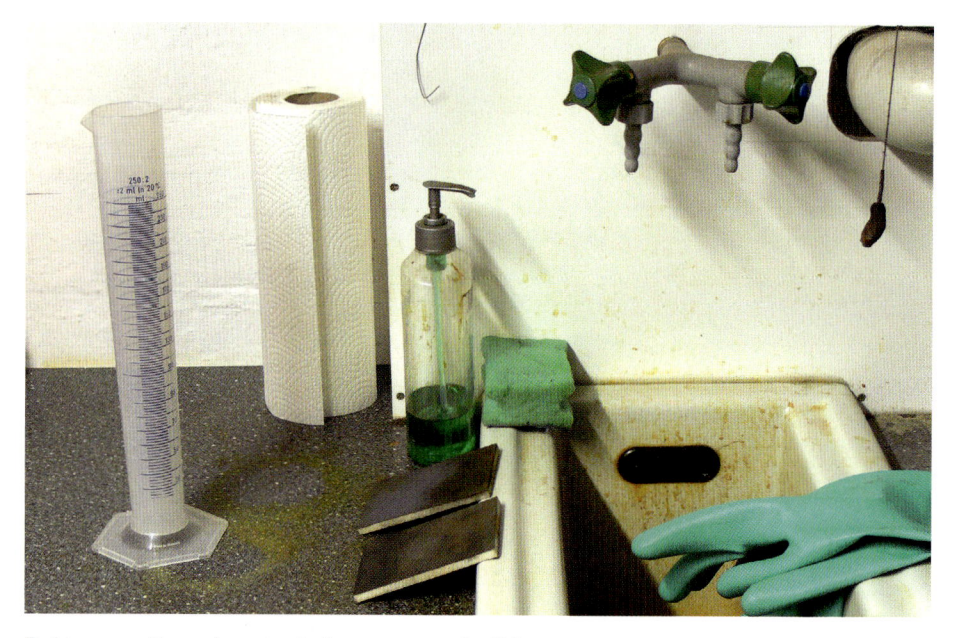

Etching utensils: graduated cylinder, paper towels, dish soap, sponge, gloves, Micro-Mesh, magnet on a wire.

Chapter 19: Working with Damascus

etching pattern is created around the contact areas, make sure your pull wire is attached to a part of the workpiece that won't be visible in the finished project (e.g., the tang of a knife).

If the object doesn't provide such a location, a magnet attached to a wire can be helpful. To keep the magnet from scratching the surface of the workpiece, wrap it in duct tape. Thus objects without a "hook" can be deposited in the acid and taken out again. The magnet should be detached from the object during the etching process to avoid irregularities of the etching around the contact area.

After the object has been removed from the acid, neutralize and rinse it thoroughly. Immediately after the first submersion in acid, the workpiece ought to be removed and checked. If marked differences in brightness or streaks show up in the etching, there are still residues of fat or detergent on the surface. To repeat this test during the next try, remove the dark hue by rubbing the piece with steel wool (extra fine, number 000). The object should again be freed from fat and rinsed.

If the etching is consistent, submerge the workpiece in the acid again and leave it there for the desired time (see chapter 9.2). When using $FeCl_3$, after a few minutes a malodorous, black coating forms on the surface of the piece. Remove this layer with a sponge or fine steel wool under running water so that subsequent etching will proceed considerably faster.

19.8 Care & Maintenance

Because the materials used to make forge-welded Damascus have a tendency to corrode, pieces should be kept slightly oiled all the time. This prevents tarnishing from sweaty palms and fruit acids to a certain degree. Nevertheless, it is a must to always clean knife blades after use and to oil them again to avoid tarnishing.

After the final etching round or polish, dry the project immediately and oil it. Completely free of fat and moist as it is, you can watch the creation of a reddish sheen. Here, it is advisable to keep oil and work cloths for oil away from the etching utensils (gloves, sponges, polishing media, cloth for drying, etc.) so there is not a risk of having fatty spots permanently etched on the workpiece.

You should use oil that is free from acid and doesn't turn into resin. Some effective oils include camellia oil, which is very reliable for protecting against corrosion and gives the surface a soft sheen. Also, a small amount goes a long way. This oil is safe and food grade; it can also be used to treat wood.

Tip

- Rub the workpiece with ample camellia oil immediately after the final etching / finish (use a soft, lint-free piece of cloth).

- Remove the excess oil about one to three minutes later.

- Let it dry.

Epilogue

The hope is that the theoretical and practical aspects introduced in this book illustrate the endless variety of Damascus steel. Nevertheless, this title can't be more than an overview attempting to impart basic knowledge. It is thus meant as an invitation to make Damascus your own by practical experiments and theoretical research.

Damascus steel offers a wide area of activity to all those who have fun trying things out and learning. When the basic techniques have been mastered, your creativity will be unlimited as you unlock and explore the wide variety of pattern techniques and variations in the process of making Damascus steel. Technical challenges are part of the daily agenda and shouldn't lead to discouragement, but rather be approached as incentives.

In conclusion, I once again want to encourage you to share the results of your own experiments, knowledge, tips, and tricks with others—only by exchanging experiences can we succeed in increasing our common knowledge and expertise with this material.

Appendix

Materials and Heat Treatment

Material	Material No.	AISI/ ASTM	DIN	Color[1]	Weldability	Availability[2]	Soft annealing Temp °F (°C)	Hardening Temp °F (°C)	Quenching Medium	Annealing Temp °F (°C)
Tool Steel	1.2842	O2	90MnCrV8		+	+	1,260–1,330 (680–720)	1,450–1,510 (790–820)	oil	340–390 (170–200)
Spring Steel	1.1231	1070	C67S		0	+	1,200–1,275 (650–690)	1,500–1,550 (815–845)	oil	575–930 (300–500)[4]
Spring Steel	1.1274	1095	C100S		0	+	1,185–1,330 (640–680)	1,440–1,490 (780–810)	oil	810–930 (430–500)[4]
File Steel	1.2206	–	140CrV1		–	+	1,310–1,360 (710–740)	1,420–1,475 (770–800)	oil[3]	215–300 (100–150)
File Steel	1.2833	W2	100V1		–	+	1,350–1,400 (730–760)	1,440–1,510 (780–820)	oil[3]	360–540 (180–280)
Ball-Bearing Steel	1.3505	52100	100Cr6		–	+	1,435–1,500 (780–800)	1,500–1,530 (800–830)	oil	300–340 (150–170)
Spring Steel	1.5026	9255	55Si7		– –	+	1,185–1,330 (640–680)	1,510–1,600 (820–870)	oil	360–390 (180–200)
Mild Steel	1.0037	–	S235 (St37)		+	+ +	–	–	–	–
Tool Steel	1.2796	15N20	75Ni8		+	–	1,200–1,290 (650–700)	1,500–1,530 (800–830)	oil	340–390 (170–200)
Tool Steel	1.2713	L6	55NiCrMoV6		–	0	1,200–1,290 (650–700)	1,530–1,600 (830–870)	oil	320–570 (160–300)
Tool Steel	1.2767	–	X45NiCrMo4		–	0	1,130–1,200 (610–650)	1,544–1,600 (840–870)	oil	340–390 (170–210)
Pure Nickel	2.4060	–	–		0	–	–	–	–	–

1) This depends on the combination of materials as well as the etching medium and duration. The depicted colors ought to be a means of comparison of the materials. Here O2 and pure nickel were used as the ends of the spectrum.

2) This evaluation is a combination of actual availability (delivered in small amounts and useful shapes) and price. A positive entry stands for good availability and low price, since these factors are usually related.

3) For these steels, water is usually mentioned as a quenching medium in the steel tables. However, especially for small cross-sections such as knife blades, oil minimizes the risk of cracks.

4) This temperature range, given for annealing springs, is probably lower for knife blades. The author estimates the annealing temperature to be 360–390°F (180–200°C) for blades.

Bibliography

Author	Title	Place	Year	Topics
Bergland, H.	*Die Kunst des Schmiedens*	Bruckmühl, Germany	2004	Practice: Extended "forging course" many special techniques
Billgren, P. + M.	*Damasteel Handbook*	Söderfors, Sweden	1999	Damasteel: methods of production, treatment, patterns
Denig, H.	*Alte Schmiedekunst Damaszenerstahl, Vol.I*	Trippstadt, Germany	1990	Damascus: history, technical basics, working techniques
	Alte Schmiedekunst Damaszenerstahl, Vol. II	Trippstadt, Germany	1999	Damascus: working techniques, pattern creation, producing bloomery steel
Hrisoulas, J.	*The Pattern-Welded Blade: Artistry in Iron*	Boulder, Colorado	1994	Practice: Forge-welded Damascus, pattern creation
Kapp, L. + H. Yoshihara, Y.	*The Craft of the Japanese Sword*	New York, New York	1987	Theory: forging and polishing Japanese blades, production of mountings
Landes, R.	*Messerklingen und Stahl, 2nd edition*	Bruckmühl, Germany	2006	Theory: cutting, sharpness, blade steels, heat treatment
Midgett, S.	*Mokume Gane*	Bruckmühl, Germany	2005	Theory and practice of *Mokume gane*
Sachse, M.	*Alles über Damaszener Stahl*	Bremerhaven, Germany	2005	Damascus: reference book
	Damaszener Stahl – Mythos	Düsseldorf, Germany	2008	Damascus: history and theory
Wegst, C.W. and M. Wegst	*Stahlschlüssel Taschenbuch, 22nd edition*	Marbach, Germany	2010	Composition and characteristic heat treatment values of steels

Index

	theory	practice
A		
acids (also see etching media)	94	
aesthetic appearance	36	
annealing	166	
applying flux	107	
B		
bloomery furnace	29	
borax	93	
Bulat	33	
C		
cable Damascus	51	125
carbon content	80	
carbon diffusion	81	
chromium content	16, 33	82
coal forge	84	
composite blades	64	
cover layer technique	63	156
crucible Damascus	19	
cutting	160	

	theory	practice
citric acid	95	
D		
Damascus	10	
Damasteel	19	
damaszieren	23	
dambrascus	25	
deformation	60	148
design possibilities	41	
E		
electric oven	88	
embossing technique	58	140
etching	41-42	
etching media (also see acids)	94	
explosion pattern Damascus	60	125
F		
false Damascus	21	
ferric chloride	94	167
fire arms	31	

Index

	theory	practice
folding	129	
forge-welded Damascus	16	
forging	159	
forging flaws	115	
forging qualities	80	
forging temperature	80	110
flux	107	
G		
gas forge	86	
glass sand	93	
grinding	164	
H		
handheld hammer	90	
handle	102	
hardening	80	166
heat source	84	
history	27	
hydraulic press	91	
I		
Illerup-Ådal	29	
Indonesia	30	
industrial Damascus	16	
inlay technique	67	158
J		
Japan	21, 30	
K		
kris	30	
L		
laminate	46	
LaTène period	27, 29	
layers, arrangement (also see layers, number)	98	
layers, number	98, 129	133
Liège	31	
M		
machine chain	51	127
machining	163	
maidenhair Damascus	55	136
maintenance	169	
manganese content	81	
material combinations	83	
materials	80	
materials (table)	171	
meteoric iron	39	
Micro-Mesh	165	
mokume gane	23	
mosaic		
bitmap	47	118
finished pieces	51	125
jigsaw	50	124

	theory	practice
matrix	49	122
spirograph	48	120
multiplication	52	129
N		
nickel content	81	
notching technique	58	144
O		
orientation	52	
P		
packing	108	
pre-heating	106	
preparations		
preparing the billet	69	
primary pattern	19	
powder-metallurgical Damascus	16	
power hammer	90	
power source	90	
R		
refined steel	21	
S		
safety at work	78	
sandwich blade	11	
saw chain	51	127
secondary pattern	19	
soft annealing	161	
Solingen	31	
stacking	129	
stainless Damascus	33	
steel types	80	82
structure	36	
structure-creating technique	44	
structure-influencing technique	44	
sulfuric acid	94	
superconductive wiring	25	
surface manipulation	58	140
T		
tamahagane	21	
tertiary pattern	21	
timascus	24	
twisting	55	134
U		
unfolding	61	154
W		
wootz	19	
wyrmfāh Damascus	66	

Other Schiffer Titles

Basic Knife Making: From Raw Steel to a Finished Stub Tang Knife. Ernst G. Siebeneicher-Hellwig and Jürgen Rosinski. Learn the craft of knifemaking. 205 color images and step-by-step instructions provide for all stages of construction, from selection of the steel, to forging the blade, assembling the handle, and constructing a holder.

Size: 8 1/2" x 11"   205 color images   112 pp.
ISBN: 978-0-7643-3508-2   soft cover $29.99

The Lockback Folding Knife: From Design to Completion. Peter Fronteddu and Stefan Steigerwald. Create your own folding knife with lockback design. The fit, combination, and variety of shapes of each knife are always a new challenge and presented here in clear, easy-to-understand, step-by-step instructions with 236 color images.

Size: 8 1/2" x 11"   236 color images   112 pp.
ISBN: 978-0-7643-3509-9   soft cover $29.99

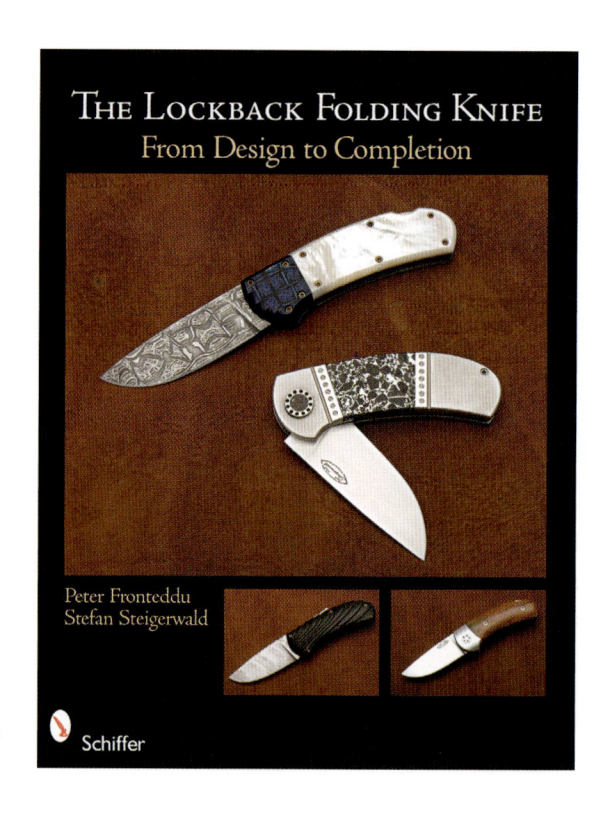

Other Schiffer Titles

Pocketknife Making for Beginners. Stefan Steigerwald & Peter Fronteddu. Make your own folding pocketknife with this easy-to-follow guide. Step by step, this instructional manual unfolds the secrets of constructing a slip joint folding knife, which is held open by spring force and friction. From template to detailed, step-by-step explanations to the finished knife, even beginners can master this project with minimal tool requirements.

Size: 6" x 9"   275+ photos & diagrams   128 pp.
ISBN: 978-0-7643-3847-2   spiral bound $29.99

Making Integral Knives. Peter Fronteddu & Stefan Steigerwald. Through step-by-step instructions and images, three integral knife projects with varying levels of difficulty are explained here. From basic patterns and principles to technical solutions to several variations in design and process, this guide is ideal for the intermediate to advanced knifemaker.

Size: 6" x 9"   350 photos & diagrams   144 pp.
ISBN: 978-0-7643-4011-6   spiral bound $24.99

Other Schiffer Titles

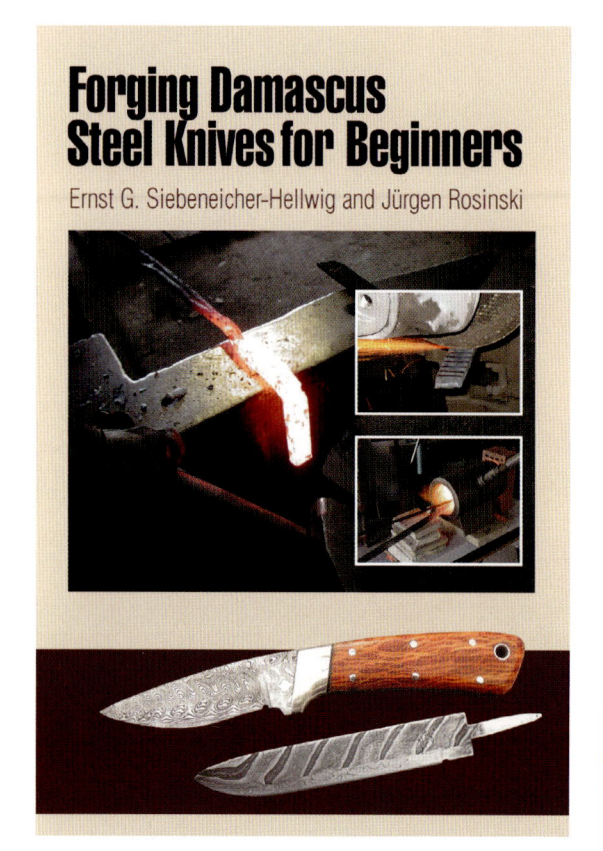

Forging Damascus Steel Knives for Beginners. Ernst G. Siebeneicher-Hellwig & Jürgen Rosinski. With this guide, novice blacksmiths and bladesmiths have a practical and budget-consious approach to forging their own Damascus steel knives. Starting with the basics, this practical guide shows how easy it can be to build a simple Damascus-grade forge; forge Damascus steel into different patterns; and forge a blade into shape, harden it, and turn it into a finished knife.

Size: 6" x 9"   180+ photos & diagrams   102 pp.
ISBN: 978-0-7643-4012-3   spiral bound $24.99

Making Hidden Tang Knives. Heinrich Schmidbauer & Hans Joachim Wieland. This beginner-level, how-to guide explains step by step how to make a fixed-blade hidden tang knife and a matching leather scabbard. Knifemakers will find the 200+ photos and diagrams, the tools and materials lists, and the detailed instructions perfectly suited to creating this knife.

Size: 6" x 9"   200+ photos & diagrams   108 pp.
ISBN: 978-0-7643-4014-7   spiral bound $24.99